South Essex
Edited by Aimée Vanstone

First published in Great Britain in 2007 by:
Young Writers
Remus House
Coltsfoot Drive
Peterborough
PE2 9JX
Telephone: 01733 890066
Website: www.youngwriters.co.uk

All Rights Reserved

© Copyright Contributors 2007

SB ISBN 978-1 84602 966 0

Foreword

Young Writers was established in 1991 and has been passionately devoted to the promotion of reading and writing in children and young adults ever since. The quest continues today. Young Writers remains as committed to the nurturing of poetic and literary talent as ever.

This year's Young Writers competition has proven as vibrant and dynamic as ever and we are delighted to present a showcase of the best poetry from across the UK and in some cases overseas. Each poem has been selected from a wealth of *Little Laureates* entries before ultimately being published in this, our sixteenth primary school poetry series.

Once again, we have been supremely impressed by the overall quality of the entries we have received. The imagination, energy and creativity which has gone into each young writer's entry made choosing the poems a challenging and often difficult but ultimately hugely rewarding task - the general high standard of the work submitted ensured this opportunity to bring their poetry to a larger appreciative audience.

We sincerely hope you are pleased with this final collection and that you will enjoy *Little Laureates South Essex* for many years to come.

Contents

Braeside School
Victoria Silton (10)	1
Lily Blackwell (11)	1
Sophia Colkett (10)	2
Alexandra Pinagli (10)	2
Yasmin Badat (10)	3
Siân Blom (10)	3
Farah Panesar (10)	4
Arooj Mirza (10)	5

Crays Hill Primary School
Tammy Sheridan (11)	6
Gabrielle Egan (10)	6
Montanya Flynn (10)	7
Charlene Gammell (10)	7

Down Hall Primary School
Jack Long (10)	8
Hannah Stone (9)	8
Rosie Mackrow (9)	9
Eve Sweeney (9)	9
Caitlin Harris (10)	10
Harry Sanderson (10)	10
Millie Johnson (10)	11
Christopher Monaghan (10)	11
Max Roberts (9)	12
Jack Hardingham (9)	12
Luke Bailey (10)	13

Downham Primary School
Robyn Lewis (9)	13

Dr Walkers CE Primary School
Evie Bartlett (9)	14
Demi Cato (9)	14
Ellie-Mae Buck (9)	15
Jonathan Minihane (9)	15
Aimée Bird (7)	16

Callum Wood (8) — 16
Anthony Fordham (10) — 16
Charlotte Savill (8) — 17
Alfie Grant (9) — 17
Sam Apperley (9) — 17
Mitchell Tunnard (8) — 18
Charlotte Heaney (8) — 18
Jack Brown (8) — 18
Rhys Harvey (8) — 19
Taram Orubo (7) — 19
Dillon Twitchett (8) — 20
Georgina Jones (9) — 20
Henry Marsh (7) — 21
Lucy Warren (9) — 21
Niamh Gough (9) — 21
Emily Hulme (7) — 22
Stuart Kerwin (7) — 22
Poppy Lawrance (7) — 23
Conor Edwards (7) — 23
Madeleine Fox (8) — 24
Molly Edghill-Lane (7) — 24

Gidea Park College

Tony Lopez (9) — 25
Jack Negus (10) — 26
Hashleen Kataria (9) — 27
Kulveer Mangat (9) — 28
Sam Hayes (10) — 29
Jack Farey (9) — 30
Charlotte Vallance (10) — 30
Lewis Jones (10) — 31
Renee Jacques (9) — 32
Grace Hamberger (9) — 33
Siddharth Subramaniam (10) — 34
Alex Loucaides (10) — 35
Ryan Siabi (10) — 36
Sonam Patel (10) — 37
Adrian Yong (9) — 38
Amy Woods (9) — 39
Fahad Masood (10) — 40
Lucy Ingram (9) — 41

Evan Pheby (9) 42
Oliver Portway (10) 43

Herington House School
Laurence Green (9) 44
Sharmilan Sivakumaran (10) 45
Simran Goyal (10) 46
Katie Corcoran (10) 47
Grace Langley (10) 48
Abigail Wise (10) 48
Daniel Heartshorne (11) 49
Mavina Bhatta (10) 49
Josie Urry (10) 50
Elizabeth Harris (9) 51
Eleanor Marshell (10) 52
Millie Whittaker (10) 53
Raheel Tharmaraj (10) 54
Georgina Dowles (9) 55
Kennedy Jackson (11) 56
Sophie Thwaites (11) 56
Annabel Hoeffler (10) 57

Highlands Primary School
Maariyah Omar (10) 58
Tahera Begum Uddin (10) 58
Indeep Rehal (8) 59
Ifran Nizam (8) 59
Iman Khan (9) 60
Jasneet Taak (8) 60
Niraj Kumar (9) 61
Tanjia Sultana (8) 61
Anas Essop (9) 62
Varshini Vignarajah (7) 62
Artan Miftari (7) 62
Ayesha Khizar (9) 63
Irfan Rashid (10) 63
Nigel Owusu-Addai (10) 64
Eva Mannan (9) 64
Heena Bashir (10) 65
Faraz Bashir (9) 65

Oaklands School

Seshani Sritharan (9)	66
Victoria Armitage (9)	66
Matilda Brookes (9)	67
Jasmine Osmani (9)	67
Georgia Lester (9)	68
Isabella Sawtell (9)	68
Tabitha Aiken (8)	68
Tia Lineker (8)	69
Roberta Kent (8)	69
Grace Cambridge (8)	70
Benita Kaur Bahra (7)	70
Katie Andrews (7)	71
Megan Huggins (8)	71
Sonia Bhangal (8)	71
Harriet Davies (7)	72
Amber Preston (8)	72
Abbie Hembury (7)	73
Zara Rashid (7)	73
Olivia Singer (8)	74
Alexandra Williams (7)	74
Alexis Shore (8)	75
Phoebe Gibbons (8)	75
Emily Galman (7)	76

Roydon Primary School

Abbi Wren (11)	76
Ellie Woodriffe (10)	77
Theresa Dunthorne (8)	77
Antony Wren (9)	78
Rebecca Talbot (10)	78
Lucy Hancock (10)	79
Dana Moss (10)	79
Katie Bees (10)	80
Connie Maunder (11)	80
Dana McLean & Amy Hagues (10)	81
Daniel Coss (11)	81
Thomas Behr (10)	82
Mia Edgeworth (9)	83
Olivia Harding (8)	83
Katie Obeney (7)	83

St Bedes RC Primary School, Chadwell Heath
Niamh Carroll (8)	84
Shona Galt (7)	85
Mia Grant (7)	86
Emma Tracy (7)	86

St James CE School, Harlow
Beatrice Stanesby (10)	86
Ellie Evans (8)	87

St Katherine's CE Primary School, Canvey Island
Holly Angel (9)	87
Jessica Lee (11)	88
Rhiannan Crace (10)	88
Reyad Nsimbi (11)	89
Jessica Gale (10)	89
Daniel Tudor (11)	89
Georgia Plumb (9)	90
Mollie Buckle (10)	90
Erin Newman (7)	91
Connor Plumb (11)	91
Jack Saunders (10)	91
Alex Bowhay (11)	92
Curtis Cramp (11)	92
Connor Garrett (10)	92
Abbie Toogood (10)	93

St Thomas of Canterbury RC Primary School, Grays
Caitlin Smith (8)	93
Erin Rydings (10)	94
Daisy Manning (9)	94
Darlletta Oduntan (10)	95
Louisa Johnson (9)	95
Georgia Akhigbe (10)	96
Catherine Abbott (10)	97
Eleanor Baker (7)	98
Nicole Young (9)	98
Rebecca Mills (10)	99
Miriam Woodburn (9)	100
Marcus Cordery (7)	100

Charley Baker (7)	100
Josef Oliver (10)	101
Ellie Beard (8)	101
Sophie Kanikuru (8)	101
Laura Grace (10)	102

Scotts Primary School

Matthew Payne (11)	102
Jordan Howell (10)	103
Esme Ware (11)	104
Megan Willis (10)	105
Rosie Howard (10)	106
Jonathan Wake (11)	107
Leona Holland (11)	108
Jasmine Elliston (11)	109

Thorpedene Junior School

Rosie Stowe (8)	109
Carmen Ng (11)	110
Kirsty Whitfield (10) & Paige Lewis (11)	110
Hannah Vinten (9)	110
Paige Martin (10)	111
Ella Osborne (8)	112
Elisha Caddell (8)	112
Rebecca Bailey (11)	113
Zac Sussex (7)	113
Bethany Lewis (7)	114
Shannon Watson (11)	114
Olivia Marsh (8)	114
David Thomas (11)	115
Sarah Jayne Brewster (10)	115
Megan Smith (9)	115
Laura Joseph (8)	116

Warley Primary School

Michaela Maya Benedetti (7)	116
Sophie Painter (8)	117
Erin Thompson (8)	117

William Read Primary School
    Emily Rush (10)   118
    Rebecca Hayes (11)   119
    James Smith (10)   120
    Megan Blackwell (9)   120

The Poems

A Witch's Spell

Eye of toad and wing of bat,
Paw of dog and tail of rat,
Scales from a dragon, neck of giraffe,
Horn of rhinoceros, hyena's laugh.

Mane of lion, wool from a sheep,
Shell of tortoise, whale from the deep,
Elephant's tusk, tiger's toe,
Mix it up and away you go!

Leave it to rot for seventy days,
Then bring it back in the misty haze,
Ensure the poison is green with decay . . .
Now give it to your enemies and watch them
    Fade away!

Victoria Silton (10)
Braeside School

The Three Flowers Of Spring

Blossom in the tree
Blossom on the ground
Blossom floating up and down
And floating all around

Daffodils bright and yellow
Daffodils cool and mellow
Daffodils have the colour of the sun
And floating all around

Snowdrops small and white
Snowdrops stay to the ground tight
Snowdrops stay still
And floating all around.

Lily Blackwell (11)
Braeside School

My Last Day

M y last day has finally arrived
Y ippee, yippee

L aughter is heard throughout the school
A wful fractions no more today
S imply super games to play
T ime is ticking away on my last day

D ing-a-ling-a-ling
A h yes, the bell has rung
Y ippee, now it's time for fun!

Sophia Colkett (10)
Braeside School

My Feelings On Snow

I look outside and
The world is covered in a white blanket
White flakes fall from the white sky
Everything is quiet
Making no sound at all
Just silence.

The garden is still and quiet
Sometimes snow falls off the branch of the big oak
As its branches give way to the snow
It is very cold
But animals stay nice and warm.

Alexandra Pinagli (10)
Braeside School

Kennings Dog

Angry growler
Scary scowler

Noisy barker
Nosy parker

Stick fetcher
Ball catcher

Fast racer
Tail chaser

Dirt maker
Fun maker.

Yasmin Badat (10)
Braeside School

Kennings Dog

Messy muncher
Bone cruncher

Paw printer
Fast sprinter

Loud barker
Big larker

Hates cats
Tears mats

Sometimes sweet
Loves meat.

Siân Blom (10)
Braeside School

The Accident!

Mum's coming back, she's going to turn blue,
When she finds out I've broken the vase in the loo!
What will she do, shout or scream?
Like when the kettle is about to steam.

I was only washing my hands with the soap,
When it slipped out my hands, so I'm relying on hope!
The tension is like pulling a tooth,
Maybe I should just confess and tell her the truth.

I can hear the door opening, she's about to come in,
I've got to get rid of the evidence and throw it in the bin!
She's going to the toilet, she's noticed,
Oh no! what should I tell her? I really don't know.

'Where has the vase gone? Tell me no lies!'
'Would you believe me if it got invaded by flies?'
She gave me that look, 'Be realistic.'
'Oh, I knocked it over.' Get ready, she's going to go *ballistic*.
But to my surprise, she looked at me calmly with a smile on her face,
'Don't worry my dear, we can get it replaced. As long as it was
                                                    an accident.'
'Oh yes, it was!'
'Then don't be so worried, I'm not going to bite,
Just go to bed and forget it, alright?'

Farah Panesar (10)
Braeside School

Haunted House

Crumbling, ruined walls
Groaning from the tower,
Ghostly shapes flit through the halls
At the midnight hour.

Looking into bare rooms
Staring at the witches' brooms,
See the gleaming eyes of cats
On guard to catch the pesky rats.

Suddenly the stairs creak
The wailing banshees start to weep,
The ghost decides to show himself
Between the books on the library shelf.

The ghost throws the books everywhere
Into the dusty, misty, cobwebbed air,
Then he stops for that's enough
No one's scared, they're all too tough.

The ghost sits down and thinks very hard
And puts in the pantry poisoned lard,
When they spread it across their bread
Before they know it, they are dead!

Arooj Mirza (10)
Braeside School

Because That's What Travellers Do

I've got lots of friends
And I speak Irish
Cos that's what I do

I'm a traveller
And I live in a trailer
Cos that's what I am

We see different places
That's where we come from
Cos that's who we are

I can meet different people
It makes me happy
Cos that's what happens

I am proud to be Irish
I am proud to travel
Because that's what I am.

Tammy Sheridan (11)
Crays Hill Primary School

What Makes Me Feel Good When I Get Up In The Morning

I am a beautiful girl
I am a good dancer
My mum is on a diet
My sister is beautiful
My best mates will be kind to me
My nan and poppa will give me presents
I love to read and write
That's what makes me feel good.

Gabrielle Egan (10)
Crays Hill Primary School

I'm Happy

I'm happy with my family
I'm happy with me
I'm happy with my friends in school
I'm proud to be me.

I'm proud to be a traveller
I'm proud of where I live
I'm proud of my grandparents
Telling me how they lived.

I'm friendly and I make people happy
And I make them laugh
I like to help children in the playground
And I like to make them laugh.

Montanya Flynn (10)
Crays Hill Primary School

Because I'm Me

I'm proud to be a traveller
I have a good family
They always talk to me
They always help me
I have good friends
They are always pleased with me
Wherever they are
They phone me
Before I go to bed at night
They phone me
I like to do art
I like to paint flowers
I'm happy every day
Because I am me!

Charlene Gammell (10)
Crays Hill Primary School

Cinderella

Once upon a time, or so it's said
Cinderella was dreaming happily in her bed
When all of a sudden, through the door
Came her ugly sisters who gave a roar
'Cinderella, get up right now
Make our breakfasts and milk the cow.'
'Here is a letter,' said Cinderella
'Oh, it's from a young fella
Why do the ugly sisters always get a letter?
Maybe it's because they're better
My dear stepsisters, you're going to a ball.'
'Oh, that one with a big hall.'
One was so excited she jumped in the air
She accidentally fell on her sister's hair
They looked at Cinderella and calmly said
'If you go to the ball, you're dead.'
Cindy decided then and there
To secretly cut off her sister's hair!

Jack Long (10)
Down Hall Primary School

What Am I?

I have green needles
And I am tall.
You can put things on me
And I will not fall.
Underneath me
You will see,
There are presents for you and me.
What am I?

Hannah Stone (9)
Down Hall Primary School

Cinderella's Invitation

Once upon a time, or so it's said
Cinderella was dreaming happily in her bed
When all of a sudden, through the door
Came her ugly sisters who gave a roar.

'Cinderella, get up right now
Make our breakfasts and milk the cow.'
Cinderella got on her feet
Really, she could not bear the heat.

She went downstairs and into the kitchen
She nearly forgot to feed the chicken
When all of a sudden the post was here
The ugly sisters gave a loud cheer.

The letter was covered in silver and gold
It was from the prince, so I've been told
'An invitation, just for us
This time we're not gonna take the bus.'

Cinderella had to go to the ball
It says it's held in the prince's hall
'You're not going, no you're not
Whenever you dance you get too hot.'

Rosie Mackrow (9)
Down Hall Primary School

Presents

Presents I carry in my sack,
I visit every child in the night,
Mince pies I have too many of,
Better be good or else I won't come
Who am I?

Eve Sweeney (9)
Down Hall Primary School

Superhero Sends A Letter Home

Dear Amber,

Things have been super lately
All the boys are all over me
My invisibility works like a charm
I can help people in alarm
The X-ray vision is saving lives
My metal hand can stop knives
My identity mask is saving my life
All the bullets end up over Fife
Things like mice are on my side
I can hear the fish under the tide
Everyone cheers me on
Like a person called Tom.

A loving best friend.

Caitlin Harris (10)
Down Hall Primary School

The Traditional Cinderella

Once upon a time, or so it's said
Cinderella was dreaming happily in her bed
When all of a sudden, through the door
Came her ugly sisters who gave a roar
'Cinderella, get up right now
Make our breakfasts and milk the cow.'
Whilst Cinderella was cooking the toast
Her sisters couldn't help but boast
'You're an ugly little brat
Your hair is a mess and you're much too fat
That's why you never make it to the prince's ball like that.'
Her ugly sisters left with a giggle
Poor Cinderella in a bit of a wriggle
She saw a note and in a puff of smoke
She saw a fairy godmother sitting in a boat!

Harry Sanderson (10)
Down Hall Primary School

Cinderella

Once upon a time, or so it's said
Cinderella was dreaming happily in her bed
When all of a sudden, through the door
Came her ugly sisters who gave a roar
'Cinderella, get up right now
Make our breakfasts and milk the cow
Next you clean the whole house up
Then you can clean up the icky dog's muck
Finally, you can get the bills and the post
Then make yourself a yummy piece of toast.'

Then there was an invitation to the prince's ball
Suddenly the ugly sisters gave a great fall
'Cinderella, don't be so sad
Just because you can't go, don't feel bad
Don't worry Cindy, you clean up instead
Then go to sleep in your lovely bed.'

Millie Johnson (10)
Down Hall Primary School

Superhero Sends A Letter

Dear Dad
Things have been super lately,
No villain or criminal can defeat me.
I can run faster than any spaceships,
I am only eating NASA restaurant space chips.
My regeneration is working fine,
I only did it once when I got hit by a mine.
My hand transforming is doing just that,
But I had one little accident when I was giving someone a pat.
My sonic sword went straight through a driver,
But brought him back to life with my sonic screwdriver.
At the moment things are like this still,
We should meet up once and have a beer down at the mill.

Your loving son,
Superhero number one!

Christopher Monaghan (10)
Down Hall Primary School

Cinderella's Invitation

Once upon a time, or so it's said
Cinderella was dreaming happily in her bed
When all of a sudden, through the door
Came her ugly sisters who gave a roar
'Cinderella, get up right now
Make our breakfasts and milk the cow.'
'Here is a letter,' Cinderella said
'Don't worry, I will remember to put the butter on the bread.'
Cinderella pleaded, 'Can I go to the ball?'
'No, you can clean the wall.'
Cindy decided then and there
To secretly cut off their hair
They were both sleeping peaceful in the night
'In a couple of minutes I will give them a fright.'
Snip, snip! 'This is fun
Whoops, the clock's struck one.'
No one's going to the royal ball
Next time they will learn not to be so cruel.

Max Roberts (9)
Down Hall Primary School

The Storm

'What's making the trees fall like soldiers?'
'Hush, it's only the storm.'

'What's making the kitchen windows smash open?'
'Hush, it's only the storm.'

'Why is the wind blowing in from the west?'
'Hush my dear, it's only the storm,
Quick past darkness catching the morn
Hush my dear, it's only the storm
Cuddle up with me and you will be warm.'

Jack Hardingham (9)
Down Hall Primary School

Cinderella

Once upon a time, or so it's said
Cinderella was dreaming happily in her bed
When all of a sudden, through the door
Came her ugly sisters who gave a roar
'Cinderella, get up now
Make our breakfasts and milk the cow.'
She washed the dishes in the sink
And soon they came out glossy pink
While she was washing the rest of the dishes
The sisters forgot to feed the fishes
Cinderella heard a knock at the door
The sisters ran downstairs and shook the floor
It was a man with a shiny letter
Cinderella should have known better
The man said, 'You are invited to a ball.'
Cinderella was so excited, she started to fall
But the stepmother said, 'No, you can't come
The prince wouldn't talk to you
With that ugly little thumb.'

Luke Bailey (10)
Down Hall Primary School

The Rainforest

Rainforest, rainforest ever so tall,
Rainforest, rainforest watch me fall.

Roses, roses watch them grow,
Roses, roses watch them row by row.

Rainforest green and lush,
In all its silence, nothing but hush.

Water, water falling down,
Splish, splash to the ground.

Robyn Lewis (9)
Downham Primary School

The Amazing Weather

The sun glistens
Reflecting off the windows
The sun glistens
As it lights the rooms

The rain sparkles
As I hear its gentle patter
The rain sparkles
As it softly falls

The snow drifts down
The trees turn white
The snow drifts down
As I play in the crunchy snow

The sun glistens
The rain sparkles
The snow drifts down
What a wonderful sight!

Evie Bartlett (9)
Dr Walkers CE Primary School

Colourful Flowers

In a flowering garden
Where the air blows
Beside the pond
Where the sun glows

The beautiful flowers
Are colourful and bright
They look lovely
What a wonderful sight!

Demi Cato (9)
Dr Walkers CE Primary School

The Weather

Have you seen the silver shimmering rain,
Go down the drain?

Have you seen the white snow
That melts and starts to flow?

Have you seen the wind blow so hard
That the trees bend and creak?

Have you seen the lightning boom and crash?
It's like a fight with lightning and clouds.

Have you seen the rainbow
With bright, strong colours?

That's all the sorts of weather in England
And there is one more -
Have you seen the bright yellow sun
Licking its thumb?

Ellie-Mae Buck (9)
Dr Walkers CE Primary School

High In The Sky

High in the sky standing proud,
Is a wonderful, magnificent cloud.
It floats around gracefully
And makes the world a happier place.

High in the sky is the sun,
Shining bright so we can have fun.
It beams down from the sky
And brightens up all of the world.

Jonathan Minihane (9)
Dr Walkers CE Primary School

Snow

I went out in the snow and I saw it glow,
I went out in the snow and I saw it blow,
I went out in the snow and I saw it so,
I like the snow because it glows and it blows,
Snow is fantastic, sometimes it glows,
Snow is white and it will never change because it glows,
I like snow that glows, snow glow, never stop glowing,
Never stop little snowflakes,
Snow keep falling, never stop,
Look at it glow, it looks so unique.

Aimée Bird (7)
Dr Walkers CE Primary School

Under The Sea

Under the sea
I see the turtle and the squid
I see the crab and the angelfish
I see the ray and the crayfish
I see the starfish having his lunch
I see a pufferfish eating his tea
I see killer whales and sharks coming after me
'Help! Help!' But no one came
So they came up to me and gobbled me up!

Callum Wood (8)
Dr Walkers CE Primary School

The Beach

Under the sea there are crabs clapping
And seaweed flapping.
The sea's going up and the shells are going down,
The sun's beating down and the ice cream's melting.
The seagulls are swooping down from the sky.

Anthony Fordham (10)
Dr Walkers CE Primary School

The Mermaid

Quick flashes of colours,
Blue, purple, red, wavy yellow.
Did I hear a splash near the cove?
What's that on the rocks?
Quick look! No, it's gone.
What's that jumping out of the water?
Surely it couldn't be a mermaid.
What's that coming nearer?
It's got hair, it's got a tail,
Be careful, it might bite!
Wow! It's a mermaid!

Charlotte Savill (8)
Dr Walkers CE Primary School

Horrible Histories

Rough and tough
It's about a long time ago
Cavemen, dinosaurs and stuff
London burned, many people got hurt
Germans invaded England with planes
Romans came on foot to battle
There were no alarm clocks to wake us up.

Alfie Grant (9)
Dr Walkers CE Primary School

Bloodthirsty Ferrets

Some ferrets are nasty and fat
They are only fat because they eat other animals
Just last week I caught one attacking next-door's cat
He won the most vicious cat award!

Sam Apperley (9)
Dr Walkers CE Primary School

The Beautiful Earth

All the beauty on the Earth
In the sea you can always surf
The sunflower in the summer
You could always be a runner
All the juicy and soft fruit
And men can go to work in a suit
All the birds flying around
And sometimes they land on the ground.

Mitchell Tunnard (8)
Dr Walkers CE Primary School

Gymnastics

Gym is fun
I like gymnastics
We do jumping, backbends,
Cartwheels, handstands and
Roly-poly on the floor.

Gymnastics is fantastic
Bar, beam and trampolining.

Charlotte Heaney (8)
Dr Walkers CE Primary School

007

James Bond is a secret spy
His spy name is 007
He has a new Bentley
It has lots of gadgets
He has a helicopter
It has five guns
007, you're the best.

Jack Brown (8)
Dr Walkers CE Primary School

The Graceful Garden

The birds dance and twirl
And so do I
The moon glimmers in the sky
The birds sing beautifully
The fish jump from the water
They fly over the moon
The horses run through the night
I see a bird of blinding beauty
The pond sparkles
There is a person that dances
I hope that it's my one true love
The bees flutter in the sky
The flowers bloom into the most beautiful of all
The cherry blossom shines gracefully
The greatest of all things is the planets.

Rhys Harvey (8)
Dr Walkers CE Primary School

Treasure Boxes

I once dug up a treasure box,
So then I started to measure,
I saw some money,
Then I started to eat honey,
I spent some money on clothes,
Then I started to doze,
Wake up, wake up, it's time to shop,
Well, well, I need to hop,
I had a new house, it's so cool,
It's even got a swimming pool,
I've still got money, what should I do?
But there's only enough for me and you,
Spend, spend, spend, spend,
Here's my receipt, I need a pen!

Taram Orubo (7)
Dr Walkers CE Primary School

Harrods

Harrods is one of the biggest shops in the world.
What can it be like?
Posh, rock and roll, pet shop and even a toy shop.
Could it be a whole variety?
It is run by Mohamed Al Fayed.
Could it be a magical land?
Could it be pretty or crowded?
Can it have food?
It can be wonderful.
It has almost anything: books, guitars, drums,
Animals, toys, food.
Harrods, Harrods, it is a beautiful shop.
Can it be lovely?
Could there be famous football players,
Rugby players, or even tennis players . . .
Signing things?
Harrods is a beautiful place.

Dillon Twitchett (8)
Dr Walkers CE Primary School

Under The Sea

Under the sea,
What do you see?
A starfish on the seabed,
The colour of orange and red.

Under the sea,
What do you see?
A dolphin jumping in the sea,
It is such a surprise for me.

Under the sea,
What do you see?
The sparkling green of the sea,
It was such a shock for me.

Georgina Jones (9)
Dr Walkers CE Primary School

Genie In A Lamp

I had a lamp.
I rubbed the lamp.
A genie came out.
I had three wishes.
I wished I was a dodgeball player
And had a big house
And that the genie went back in the lamp.
Ha ha!

Henry Marsh (7)
Dr Walkers CE Primary School

The Dolphins

Under the sea are smooth, glistening creatures
They are intelligent
When you least expect it, they leap into the air!
It's like a swan flying
They slowly swish their tails from side to side
When they see some fish, *snap!* They are gone.

Lucy Warren (9)
Dr Walkers CE Primary School

My Woodland Poem

Orange of the leaves falling off the trees
Green of the grass pushing up from the ground
Blue of the bluebells drooping down
Lump of the anthills, oh I tripped over it!
A man cut down a tree, lovely, rough and brown.

Niamh Gough (9)
Dr Walkers CE Primary School

My Dwarf Hamsters

My dwarf hamsters are very small,
They are cool,
The way they move,
Small, small animals are cool,
They move around a lot faster when they're small,
Hamsters, hamsters like to laugh,
They also have a glass,
I bet you didn't know what they are,
But I hope you do now,
But in case you don't, I'll explain a bit more,
They like scratching by their door,
They like burying themselves under the sawdust,
Then go to sleep.

Emily Hulme (7)
Dr Walkers CE Primary School

Over The Mountain

I saw a mountain
It had some sugar on the top of it
And it was nice
So I started to climb the mountain
And when I got to the top
It was slippery
And I forgot my slippery board
So I slid down the mountain
And fell over a rock
And hurt my back.

Stuart Kerwin (7)
Dr Walkers CE Primary School

Weather

At Christmas, Santa comes and gives you holly
And makes you jolly.
Springtime comes,
Baby lambs are born
And lambs are shorn.
When it is summer,
I like a bunny.
When it is summer,
The bees make honey.
When it is autumn,
The leaves fall into a pool.

Poppy Lawrance (7)
Dr Walkers CE Primary School

Boxing Time

One day there was a boy called Conor
He was a boxer
He loved to spar
His dad said, 'You'll go far
And win the Golden Gloves!'

Finally, it was the day
Conor was on his way

Conor had three rounds
He won!
He brought the Golden Gloves to school
And everyone was proud.

Conor Edwards (7)
Dr Walkers CE Primary School

The Four Seasons Of The Year

Spring, spring, it's here again,
The best time to make a den,
Here we go, back to school,
I hope it's really cool, cool, cool.

Summer, summer, it's here again,
I'm off school there and then,
Playing with my brothers now,
Whipping up with a towel.

Autumn, autumn, it's here again,
Running and playing in the leaves,
I am always falling,
Down on my knees.

Winter, winter, it's here again,
Throwing snowballs at your friends,
My mum is making delicious food,
I hope it makes me feel good, good, good.

Madeleine Fox (8)
Dr Walkers CE Primary School

School

School, school, school is cool,
Always has a swimming pool.
You'll have so much fun,
They make hot cross buns.
You have friends to play every day,
You will love Dr Walkers, you really will.
No laws, no claws in the country, not here,
You have Mrs Stoker who helps us learn,
Never lets the school burn,
We have all our classes right here.

Molly Edghill-Lane (7)
Dr Walkers CE Primary School

The Wreck Of The Dominican Isle

Up came the waves
Breaking the deck,
The mighty ship was
Turned into a wreck.

The waves crashed down
As the crew screamed,
The ship was upturned
Into the sea.

The ship came up
Once again,
But the storm became worse
As it started to rain.

Up came the waves
Breaking the deck,
The mighty ship was
Turned into a wreck.

The mighty ship was
Finally beaten,
The ship was alight
Just like a beacon.

As the ship was devoured
By the sea,
The storm was calmed
Just like me.

Up came the waves
Breaking the deck,
The mighty ship
Was turned into a wreck!

Tony Lopez (9)
Gidea Park College

The Wreck Of The Madagascar III

The wind is roaring
The sea is crashing
Wood is snapping
People are shouting

Here comes the wreck of the Madagascar
The wreck of the Madagascar draws closer
The sails white against the dark sky
Water crashing over the broken hull

The wind is roaring
The sea is crashing
Wood is snapping
People are shouting

Wood screaming as it hits the rocks
People dying
Waves smashing at the hull
Rocks piercing through the hull

The wind is roaring
The sea is crashing
Wood is snapping
People are shouting

The shouting stops
The screaming stops
The ship is in its watery grave!

Jack Negus (10)
Gidea Park College

The Wreck Of The Montego Bay II

T he wreck of the Montego Bay
H appened sadly on this day
E xactly as the capt'n feared

W ind drove them, however they steered
R ight upon the ragged rocks
E arly splintered the decks
C rashing the keel while it splintered
K aput! She soon was shattered

O ver she rolled, the grand old lady
F alling ropes, sails and cargo

T ipping into the raging spume
H eadlong toppling came the crew
E nding up in the water

M en whose lives soon grew shorter
O n the beach their bodies washed
N othing could be done to save them
T hough the locals came to watch
E arly this disaster could have altered
G oing west instead of east
O r

B iding our time in the last port
A nd waiting for the storm to cease or
Y ield.

Hashleen Kataria (9)
Gidea Park College

The Wreck Of The Madagascar II

On the little Cornish isle,
There was a ship about a mile
Out to sea,
'Wreck!' came the cry from down below
And up above.

Crash, crash, boom, bash!

The ship was coming in closer,
Now you could see it was in peril,
The waves lashed up and crashed upon the stern.

Crash, crash, boom, bash!

The wind blew the ship in closer and closer,
Towards the rocks.
Lightning struck, lighting up the dark sky,
Revealing its name, Madagascar.

Crash, crash, boom, bash!

The little ship was dead for sure,
The men desperately tried to turn it around,
But luck was against them.

Crash, crash, boom, bash!

The ship's stern was crushed
By an enormous wave
And at last it met its end.

Crash, crash, boom, bash!

Kulveer Mangat (9)
Gidea Park College

The Wreck Of The Cuban Isle

The Cornish rocks await the ship
That comes fast upon them from the sea
Which crashes and roars as the wind screams
And rolls over the deck and me!

'Wreck! Wreck!' the Cornishmen shout
The white sails against the dark blue sky.

'No! No!' the men shout
As the mast snaps in two
Ropes flap, sails rip, seas roar
And roll over the deck towards you.

'Wreck! Wreck!' the Cornishmen cry
The white sails against the dark blue sky.

Run, run, but you cannot hide
From the crashing waves above
The waves lap against the ship's side
And drive the hull with a shove.

'Wreck! Wreck!' the Cornishmen cry
The white sails against the dark blue sky.

The great ship Cuba has been destroyed
And everything has gone away
Men dead, the mast snapped
And everything has gone quiet.

'Wreck! Wreck!' the Cornishmen cry
The white sails against the dark blue sky.

Sam Hayes (10)
Gidea Park College

The Wreckage Of Madagascar

The storm was scary, terrifying,
Everyone was shouting, 'Wreck, wreck!'
The wind was bellowing, the sails were flapping.

'Help, help!' someone shouted on the boat,
As the boat was getting closer to the rocks.

The lightning and thunder crashed overhead
And the boat was getting closer to overflowing.

'Help, help!' someone shouted on the boat,
As the boat was getting closer to the rocks.

Bang! The ship hit the rocks
And the bow got damaged again.
Everyone was screaming with fear.

'Help, help!' someone shouted on the boat,
As the boat was getting closer to the rocks.

Jack Farey (9)
Gidea Park College

The Wreck Of The Jamaican Lad

The sea is lashing,
The waves are crashing,
In this windy and thundering storm.

The boat is slipping,
The sails are ripping,
In this windy and thundering storm.

There is hissing and groaning
And roaring and moaning,
In this windy and thundering storm.

There are cheers and more,
As they get to shore,
In this windy and thundering storm.

Charlotte Vallance (10)
Gidea Park College

The Wreck Of The Martinique

T hundery weather clashing
H owling winds whistling
E ar-piercing screams from the crew

W renching ropes breaking
R oaring waves crashing
E ndless yelling for help
C ascading water
K notting ropes tangling

O ff the coast of Dover
F ierce bellowing from the captain

T he lightning flashing
H urtling rain lashing
E ars of the crew popping

M oaning from the captain
A nd the splintering wood
R ound the coast of Dover
T earing waves breaking the bough spit
I n the dangerous waters
N o! The ship's capsized
I n the water she goes
Q uick, haul the lifeboat
U pon the water lay the crew
E nding for them all.

Lewis Jones (10)
Gidea Park College

The Wreck Of The Malabar

The bellow of the wind
And the patter from the rain,
Made the bow of the Malabar,
Wallow in the waves.

It could not take any more,
Of the heavy, cascading waves,
As it tried to stay upright,
For us to sail it once again.

The wind was howling,
The sea was pounding away,
Like a big, scary monster,
Waiting for its prey.

The rain beat upon the deck
And madly began to pour,
We all knew that this was a wreck,
We knew that for sure.

The people began to scream,
The boat began to rock,
Suddenly, a massive crunch
And everyone was in shock.

Renee Jacques (9)
Gidea Park College

The Wreck Of The Malabar III

T he crashing of the waves hit against the rocks.
H owling winds threw the boat to and fro.
E veryone on the boat was crying for help.

W aves flew over the boat,
R oaring winds blew as the heavens opened.
E vil spirits pushed the boat on her side.
C rashing, howling, moaning of the passengers
K aput pieces of the boat sinking in the sea.

'O verboard, overboard, someone has gone overboard,'
  said the captain.
F og started to cover the coast.

T errible, sharp cries floated away.
H ere and there people tugged the ship
'E asy,' the people thought, 'this is not.'

M yself, I was standing on the rocks.
A mongst the waves I saw someone
L ying in the water.
A round people screaming.
B ellowing winds.
A last scream from the noble ship
R olling on her side.

Grace Hamberger (9)
Gidea Park College

The Wreck Of The Malabar II

The churning sea swaying the ship,
Spraying the deck
And making the sailors slip.

The bellowing wind, the pellets of rain,
Pushing the ship
To the rocky terrain.

The murky mist, the flashes of lightning,
The lashing water
Made it all quite frightening.

The towering waves, the strong gale
And the icy water
Made all the crew wail.

The ship plunged down under a massive wave,
Taking the crew into what seemed
A gigantic cave.

The ship sank to the seabed,
Motionless and eerie
And the sailors all lay dead.

Siddharth Subramaniam (10)
Gidea Park College

The Wreck Of The Endeavour

As the Endeavour crashes along,
Along the beachy rocks, storm, hail,
Rain and snow, crying, shouting and
Screaming.

Oh, oh, the Endeavour crashing along the rocks,
Everybody dying for help, oh, oh, oh.

'Cap'n, cap'n, wreck, wreck,'
Cry the bosun and the mate,
And praying for God to help them to
Avoid this terrible fate.

Oh, oh, the Endeavour crashing along the rocks,
Everybody dying for help, oh, oh, oh.

As the ship capsizes
On the briny sea,
The bodies of the dead shipmates
Bob about for all to see.

Oh, oh, the Endeavour crashing along the rocks,
Everybody dying for help, oh, oh, oh.

Alex Loucaides (10)
Gidea Park College

The Wreck Of The Dominica

As the ship came closer and closer
To the sharp teeth of the rocks
Out of the ship came
Loud screams crying for help.

It was hard to hear
As the ship ripped with a screaming bellow.
There was a loud crash
As the weak ship capsized against the rocks.

The bitter lashing of the angry waves
Slapping and snapping,
Tearing the ship
Into tiny fragments of paper.

There was no chance
For the splintering ship,
Crashing and smashing against the rocks
Sinking deep below the sea.

Ryan Siabi (10)
Gidea Park College

The Wreck Of The Cuba

The wind bitter and cold
Roaring and whistling
The Cuba was beating upwind
Desperate to reach the harbour soon.

The cry went all around
The Cuba was coming closer in
Waves flooding and ripping
Black storm clouds came.

The men screeching and yelling
As hail came down
The ship was moving side to side
Not knowing when it would crash.

A massive wave broke over her stern
There were more shouts and cries
The Cuba didn't come upright again
The wonderful ship then lay on her side.

Sonam Patel (10)
Gidea Park College

The Wreck Of The Malay

The ship was sailing by
In a very windy storm
As the wind was blowing wildly
The sails were flapping like doves.

The ancient ship, Malay, sank on this day.

Rocks were coming ahead
With the lighthouse shining
The Malay couldn't stop
And the wheel kept on spinning.

The ancient ship, Malay, sank on this day.

The waves were crashing
And the mast fell,
The bow was crashing
And people were shouting, 'Wreck! Wreck!'

The ancient ship, Malay, sank on this day.

The ship was smashing into the rocks
Men were screaming for help
And the hull broke in two
The ship was wallowing in the salty seas.

The ancient ship, Malay, sank on this day.

Adrian Yong (9)
Gidea Park College

The Wreck Of Jamaica

The wind was howling,
The waves were crashing,
And the ship kept on swaying
Side to side.

Run Jamaica, run,
Sailing back to the Caribbean sun.

The thunder crashed,
The lightning flashed
And part of the boat,
Went *snap!*

Run Jamaica, run,
Sailing back to the Caribbean sun.

The sail snapped,
The ship crashed,
The ship went
Up the rocks.

Run Jamaica, run,
Sailing back to the Caribbean sun.

The people were shouting,
The lightning was flashing,
And the people were yelling,
And people were overboard.

Amy Woods (9)
Gidea Park College

The Wreck Of The Rio

As the Rio plunges forward,
The crew begin to sleep,
The waves crash over the starboard side,
The bow pushes through the waves.

Rio, oh Rio, our fine ship sails,
The waves roar and knock the ship side to side,
The lightning strikes and rages on and on for ages!

Towering waves make the Rio small,
As it swings to and fro,
As the waves hit the deck,
In the cruel and monstrous sea.

Rio, oh Rio, our fine ship sails,
The waves roar and knock the ship side to side,
The lightning strikes and rages on and on for ages!

The thunder roars,
The waves slash through the hull,
The lightning blasts,
The final wave ended the ship, charging like a bull!

Fahad Masood (10)
Gidea Park College

The Wreck Of The Amazonia

The ship was rocking side to side,
In the rushing rain,
They had seen it all before,
It was a wreck once again.

So everyone else came rushing down,
To see what was going on,
And everyone rushed to haul it out,
Before it had sunk and gone!

The feeling was extraordinary,
And everyone was glad,
That a ship had finally come,
Though it was quite sad.

Laura and her family,
Were very, very pleased,
Until someone told them,
Men were in the seas!

Everyone was trying to pull the ship ashore,
But it kept on floating back,
And the chief was getting angry,
Because he'd get the sack!

Lucy Ingram (9)
Gidea Park College

The Wreck Of The Bahamas

The winds lashing,
The sea crashing,
Men screaming,
The sails being ripped apart.

Rocks tearing the ship,
I don't know what to do,
The sea hissing and spitting,
The deck being flooded.

The waves pushing my ship to and fro,
The rain crashes down,
The wind tears into the flag,
I see a dark shadow, it was death.

My crew shout and scream,
They have no chance,
A wave crashes over the ship,
We slip into the blue.

Evan Pheby (9)
Gidea Park College

The Wreck Of The Bassalona

The waves smashed against the ship,
The cap'n cried, 'What's happening to my ship?'
The darkness loomed, the water sprayed,
I prayed to God I would be saved.

I heard the roaring from the sea,
As soon as the ship got out to sea.
It hit the rocks with a big crash,
Knocked everyone down with a big bash.

The ship was sinking, oh save us all!
We would be meeting Davy Jones for supper after all.
The wind was howling, waves were crashing,
What would become of us all?

Then out of the mist came a boat,
Its owner cried, 'Come on in, it will float.'
We sailed away, far away,
We're still alive, *hooray!*

Oliver Portway (10)
Gidea Park College

What Food Looks Like

Food has weird lookalikes
Especially carrots because
They are like Mum's fingers
They are so long and very pointy
Green beans are grass
Baked beans are stones
Sugar cubes are hailstones

Food has weird lookalikes
Especially the orange
It's like the bright sun
On a summer day

Two eggs are eyes. What are they?
Spies.
Probably they work at M Eye High.

I wonder if a vampire would devour
Tomato sauce instead of blood?
Put it on your chips
But don't make a flood.

Food has weird lookalikes
A banana is a telephone
Potatoes are rocks
Spaghetti is hair
Imagine a world that you could eat
What an extraordinary world that would be
Some mean feat.

Laurence Green (9)
Herington House School

Food

Cherries like rubies,
On the ground,
Sparkling brightly,
Which I have just found.
They've fallen from the tree
And they are just for me.

A banana like a smile,
A lemon like the sun,
A kiwi like a tennis ball,
Yet chocolates I've had none.

Also on the menu
There were sausages and chips,
The chips like fingers
And the sausages like sticks.

Spaghetti like worms,
It's also like my hair,
Crawling slowly,
Almost everywhere.

The straw in my lemonade,
Looks more like a hose,
But the tea and coffee
Are the drinks which I chose.

Food, food, what shall I do?
So many fruits and vegetables
And delicious chocolates too.

Sharmilan Sivakumaran (10)
Herington House School

The Robot

I used to be a brand new robot polished well,
Very attractive they used to tell,
In the shop I stood, well designed, nice and glossy,
But the person who made me was very bossy.

I used to be a brand new robot polished well,
Very attractive they used to tell,
The boy who brought me read the instructions upside down,
So then it all ended with a frown.

I used to be a brand new robot polished well,
Very attractive they used to tell,
Once the little boy worked out how to use me,
My personality he could see.

I used to be a brand new robot polished well,
Very attractive they used to tell,
Soon I became rusty and stiff,
Then he locked me in a cupboard
Like I became a legend or a myth.

I used to be a brand new robot polished well,
Very attractive they used to tell,
Now I am locked in the darkness all alone,
All by myself, all on my own.

I used to be a brand new robot polished well,
Very attractive they used to tell,
Now, in the cupboard all I can see,
Is a fully grown man peering at me.

Simran Goyal (10)
Herington House School

The Tattered, Battered Clown

The tattered old clown sat down in a tent,
His shoes all battered, his back all bent.

His eyes were weeping, all blurred and red,
The children used to love him and they always said,
'Come on, Mr Clown, give us a dance,'
And he always used to leap and prance.

But now he was too old to perform,
And every day he was crying and forlorn.
But wait! A man had beckoned for him to come out,
And when he did, people made a shout.

His shoes were too big, that was the only thing,
He tripped, he slipped, maybe he should sing.
He never wanted to be a silly clown performer,
He wanted to be a singer who was just round the corner.

To all the children's houses that they wanted to see,
Shall he do the Mikado, no that cannot be.
He let out a note with a very deep breath,
So perfectly clear, it could be heard by the deaf.

People gave a gasp, they started to applaud,
The clown was no longer crying and forlorn.
The clown was now famous and very well known,
He even performed in all the important shows.

The clown was now happy and content again,
His wonderful singing brought him lots of fame.
The clown went into his chamber and closed the door,
And smiled as he looked at his gleaming shoes on floor!

Katie Corcoran (10)
Herington House School

Lonely Bear

I once was a bear all fluffy and grey,
I was put into a shop and told to behave.
I started to cry, but they would not let me out,
Then a different girl picked me up, so I gave a big shout.

She took me home with all her toys,
But sadly they were all boys.
I am a girl all pretty in pink,
So I gave a twirl and made her wink.

She took all the toys from under the bed,
But I'm special too and would like to be fed.
Why did she just take the boys?
Tea parties are great for all toys!

Here I lay all tattered and torn,
Nobody wants me, I'm old and worn.
To all you children, listen and learn,
Look under your beds and give me a turn.

Grace Langley (10)
Herington House School

Sadness

Sadness is white like a lonely swan.

It tastes like stale bread that's been in the cupboard too long.
It looks like tears rolling down a sad child's cheek.
It feels like someone piercing a hole in your heart.
It smells like chocolate you're not allowed to eat.
It sounds like the wailing of a baby.

Sadness is white like a lonely swan.

Abigail Wise (10)
Herington House School

My Podgy Penguin

My podgy penguin is as heavy as a cow after grazing in a field
And as long as a guinea pig stretching in the morning.
It is as strong as a dinosaur tearing down a tree
And as slow as a tortoise running around a field.

My podgy penguin is as noisy as a guitar amplifier on full blast
And as big as a barge taking the rubbish out.
It is as gentle as a feather falling off a bird
And as greedy as a pig in a sty all day.

My podgy penguin is as happy as a dolphin jumping in the waves
And as fast as a speedboat in the Mediterranean.
It has teeth as sharp as a thorn on a holly bush
And wings as soft as a cushion on a bed.

My podgy penguin is mine, mine, mine.

Daniel Heartshorne (11)
Herington House School

The Golden Temple

The Golden Temple,
Made entirely out of gold on the outside,
Shimmering, gleaming, beautiful.
As bright as the sun beaming down on the Earth,
As large and beautiful as a palace,
It makes me smile when I see it.
As happy as a butterfly fluttering by,
The Golden Temple,
Shining, bright and splendid.

Mavina Bhatta (10)
Herington House School

How I Lost My Appetite

Fattening bacon just like a smile,
Sizzle it in a pan for just a while,
Eggs like eyes,
What a good disguise.
Big, fat sausages, not really for me,
Swimming in juice just like the sea
And so to complete this course,
You need to pile on the tomato sauce.

Now for the sweet course,
Strawberries in chocolate sauce!
It was such a delight,
Just the first bite.

Followed by mouth-watering pancakes,
That my mum makes,
With a helping of honey for me,
Supplied by the bumblebee.
It's even better, believe me,
Washed down with a cup of tea.
I gobbled it down so quickly,
Guess what? It made me feel sickly.

'Tomorrow, dear Mum,' I said,
'Please can I have toast instead?'

Josie Urry (10)
Herington House School

The Rocking Horse

I am a withered, battered, bent rocking horse,
I was once attractive, splendid, but now I'm solemn and full
of remorse.

I was loved by a boy who rode on my back,
He was kind and gentle and his name was Jack.
When the boy rode on my back, it felt as if I was riding into battle,
Up and down the hills, passing grazing cattle,
With the wind rushing through my long, beautiful mane
And the deafening noise of a passing train.
Jack was the soldier and I was his shield,
I was always there for him in case he was killed.
He was strong, he was bold,
One fine sword he would hold.

I am now obsolete and not the same,
I imagine Jack has even forgotten my name.
I have been put in a cupboard, dark and old,
With vivid memories of Jack who was bold.

I am a withered, battered, bent rocking horse,
I was once attractive, splendid, but now I'm solemn and full
of remorse.

Elizabeth Harris (9)
Herington House School

The Old Toy Box

In his room
Was an old box of toys,
Shoved in the corner,
Ready and poised.

Full of puzzles and games
And some old, broken frames,
A football, a sword, a train or two,
Some Lego, a dolly and a plane that once flew.
Some Hot Wheels for boys,
A jack-in-the-box with no noise
That was almost new!

An old, tattered ted,
A doll's broken bed,
A puppet without strings,
A rocking horse with no springs!
A toy less its squeak,
A duck less its beak,
A brimless hat,
A miaowless cat.

So there it sat,
Shoved in the corner,
Ready and waiting
For their loving, old owner.

Then there was a face,
In that cramped, old place,
Full of joy at the thought of a toy.
He opened the lid
And remembered being a kid.

Eleanor Marshell (10)
Herington House School

All Kinds Of Food

You think you know all the food you can eat,
Let's start with eggs that you can beat,
You can have them scrambled, poached or fried,
But beware of salmonella because some have died.

Bacon, pork and ham, all come from a pig,
Whereas carrots and potatoes you have to dig.
Cauliflowers look like a brain,
Cucumber is like a train.

Broccoli stands tall like a tree,
Unlike gravy that swishes like the sea.
Pumpkins like a round beach ball,
Tomatoes red, round and small.

Strawberries are sweet, red and bright,
They grow in the field day and night.
Apples and cheese you can have for lunch,
The cheese is soft but the apples crunch.

On a Friday at school we always have fish,
But I have to say it's not my favourite dish.
There's cod, skate and mackerel and many others too,
Many people like them, do you?

On Saturday I'm allowed some treats,
I can go to the shops and buy some sweets.
There's chocolate and boiled sweets, as well as some crisps,
I'm spoilt for choice, it's all such bliss.

As you can see, there are so many foods,
It's difficult to know which one to choose.
But if I had to pick my favourite one,
It would have to be a big hot cross bun!

Millie Whittaker (10)
Herington House School

The Mechanical Man

I was once ash and silver,
With eyes as big as mossy apples,
I was the Mechanical Man,
I was courageous and handsome,
But now I am only scrawny with small eyes
And not as shiny as I used to be.

My arms they clank,
My feet they stamp,
But now I can't hear any of the stamp or clank.
All I can hear is the weeping,
It is me crying, I don't work anymore.

I once had a great owner who enjoyed me a lot,
Then he bought a ballerina
With a new pink dress.
She came in and I was filled with distress,
I am now merely an unwanted possession
Sitting on a wooden shelf collecting dust.

Eventually I got thrown out of the window
And landed in a lad's hand by chance.
A lad so sweet, with a freckled face and blue eyes.
He took me into his house,
He polished me vigorously
And hocus-pocus, *bang, bang, bang!*
I turned back into that wanted Mechanical Man
I was so many years ago!

Raheel Tharmaraj (10)
Herington House School

The String Puppet Clown

I used to be in a puppet show,
I was the one with a big, red bow,
I rocked and rolled and shouted out loud,
And there were some people that just growled.

I was the king of gliding,
Then my puppeteer went into hiding,
And he became the manager of a toy shop,
He was always cleaning the shop with a mop.

Then a kind little girl came in,
At least I didn't go in the bin,
She really desperately wanted *me,*
And this is how it went you see.

She took me home
And she would always moan,
'It's okay that you always dangle,
But why do you have to be in a tangle?'

She tried and tried
And then she cried,
'Mummy, Daddy, my toy is broken.'
'We can't fix it, we have *spoken.*'

You are useless to me and all of us three,
We'll throw you under the bed,
Or even just chop off your head,
'The puppet's life was sad,' I said.

Georgina Dowles (9)
Herington House School

My Genuine Guinea Pig

My genuine guinea pig is as light as a feather falling from the
night sky,
And as fat as marshmallows dipped in chocolate.
It is as strong as the wind beating on the cold gate
And as fast as a person running the marathon.

My genuine guinea pig is as quiet as a baby sleeping peacefully,
And as small as a mouse curled up in a ball.
It is as fierce as a lion attacking his prey
And as greedy as my baby sister guzzling milk.

My genuine guinea pig is as happy as a horse when it has
reached a show,
And as sweet as a fluffy cat.
It has eyes as shiny as bouncy balls
And legs as fat as a hippo bathing.

My genuine guinea pig is mine, mine, mine.

Kennedy Jackson (11)
Herington House School

Love

Love is pink like fluffy candyfloss.

It smells as sweet as a rose swaying softly in the breeze.
It feels like silk against my skin.
It tastes like sweets all hard and chewy.
It sounds like children laughing and playing happily.
It looks like the hot sun on a summer's day.

Love is pink like fluffy candyfloss.

Sophie Thwaites (11)
Herington House School

My Magic Box
(Based on 'Magic Box' by Kit Wright)

My box is fashioned from flower petals, leather and pebbles,
With lava on the lid and spirits in the corners.
Its hinges are made from rainbows.

I will put in my box . . .

The taste of chocolate melting in your mouth
The feel of a horse
And a flower just watered.

I will put in my box . . .

The cold from melting icicles
Some happy memories
And a picture of my friends.

I will put in my box . . .

A view of the Statue of Liberty
A queen on a dolphin and a mermaid on a horse
And an Eskimo in the cold.

I will put in my box . . .

A digging, dodging dog
A newly wed couple and the last bark of an ancient dog
And a skeleton dancing around.

My box is fashioned from flower petals, leather and pebbles,
With lava on the lid and spirits in the corners.
Its hinges are made from rainbows.

Annabel Hoeffler (10)
Herington House School

Summer Holidays

Children shout hip hip hooray,
Thank goodness it's the holidays.
No more work to be done,
Lots of people lying in the sun!

The seaside is the place to be,
The lapping of the calm sea,
Children yell for their mum,
They want an ice cream in their tum!

The theme park is just as good,
Especially if you're in a daring mood.
There are water rides, roller coasters and much more,
You can go to a haunted house for a spooky tour!

Maariyah Omar (10)
Highlands Primary School

Emotions

Emotions are wonderful things.
They give you a weird kind of tingly feeling.
So many emotions to explore.

There are: happy, sad and upset,
Jealousy, kindness and madness.

Dejected, ecstatic and proud,
Grumpy, humpy and rather quite loud.
Whatever emotions you are feeling today,
Don't bottle them up,
Just let them go free!

Tahera Begum Uddin (10)
Highlands Primary School

The Monster Computer

I have a computer with eyes that are green
And very round and very mean.
Every time I press a key,
My computer growls at me.
It started to bellow
When I tried to say hello.

Once I got so scared,
I almost screamed.

I guess it doesn't like me,
So now I stay quiet
As I'm scared it'll want me for its tea.
It bit my fingertips in two,
So you'd better watch out,
Or it might eat you!

Indeep Rehal (8)
Highlands Primary School

Friends

Friends are in every corner of the world.
Trust and faith make it strong,
That's the thing that really counts.
Every friend is special,
No one wants to lose one.
If you want a new friend,
Just be warned,
You might lose another.

Ifran Nizam (8)
Highlands Primary School

A Sea So Peaceful

The sea has waves so blue and bright,
Reflecting off the sun's warm light.
Gently lapping against each rock,
Never a disturbance, never a shock.

Sudden waves swell and boil,
All because of wasted oil.
Lots of fish shriek and moan,
'It's as dangerous as a war zone!'

We all blink foolishly and wonder why,
The sea rages and gives out cries.
We can help by making changes,
Stop catching fish in little cages.

Reduce, re-use and recycle,
Don't drive on a motorcycle.
You see citizens, this all leads,
To a tranquil and peaceful, shimmering sea.

Iman Khan (9)
Highlands Primary School

Friends

A friend . . . someone who cares about you.
When you fall down, they'll pick you up,
They never tell secrets about you,
They always stick up for you.
If you have a problem, they will sort it out,
A true friend will never let you down.

Jasneet Taak (8)
Highlands Primary School

School Is Cool

School is cool, it helps you learn,
It helps you learn whenever you go.
You should only go to school
Because if you miss it, you will go down.

You go to school five days a week
And make sure you do not miss homework day!
Because homework is cool, it helps you learn,
Teachers only give you a little bit of homework on the weekend.

You only have two days off, but do not moan
Because the teachers work hard for you for your education.
If you moan, you will not be liked
Because the teachers are the best in the world!

Don't let teachers down because if you do,
You'll end up with a frown on your face.
If you have a frown, the frown will get passed on
And everyone wants a smiley face, not a frowny face!

Niraj Kumar (9)
Highlands Primary School

Friends

A friend is someone who cares about you.
Someone who you tell secrets to
And doesn't gossip.
A friend wouldn't break up with you
Unless you said something rude to her.
A friend will play with you
And stand by you every time.

Tanjia Sultana (8)
Highlands Primary School

The Beach

The beach is a fun place
The beach is a hot place.

The beach is as fun as any old thing
The beach is so hot, thanks to the sun
Some people on the beach like to run.

The people on the beach like to lie down
The people on the beach make so much sound.

When people leave the beach
It's really quiet
When people leave the beach
It's really boring.

Anas Essop (9)
Highlands Primary School

Something Strange Is Happening . . .

The seasons appear to have changed.
Birds and animals are all confused.
Tulips have begun to bloom,
The sun is not supposed to shine every day
Because it's winter.
Something strange has happened.

Varshini Vignarajah (7)
Highlands Primary School

The Spider

Look at the spider spinning its silky thread
Look at its hairy arms
Busily weaving its trap.

Artan Miftari (7)
Highlands Primary School

Friends

If you're feeling sorry or sad
If you've got a friend, things don't turn out so bad
Friends are always near
You shouldn't have any fear.

Some friends break up
They always make up
Friends are always there
They will always care.

Friends, friends, friends
Someone you like a lot
Someone who's fun
Someone to help
When things go all wrong!

Ayesha Khizar (9)
Highlands Primary School

What Happens In School

School, school, school is a fun place to go
When you step inside the time goes slow.
In school it is really fun
So go out to play in the burning hot sun.

Go to the library and take a book
Do me a favour, don't be a crook.
Share the book with everyone
But trust me, it will be really fun.

When you go back to class, it is time for lessons
But please be quiet, it is an important session.
When you finish the lesson it's time for lunch
So eat the food and hear it go *crunch!*

It's time to go home, tell Mum what you did
'Mum, I made a friend and his name is Sid!'

Irfan Rashid (10)
Highlands Primary School

The Weather

Rainy days, rainy days
The sound it makes is *plop*
And when it comes to winter
There surely is a lot.

Sunny days, sunny days
Makes the sky shine bright
When it comes to night-time
There's not a lot of light.

Stormy days, stormy days
It goes crashing through the waves
In the night and in the day
You've done a lot on Earth today.

Nigel Owusu-Addai (10)
Highlands Primary School

The Beach

I love having fun
Right above, the hot, shining sun
Different colours in the air
And the yellow sand so fair.

The blue sea
Is down below me
The sun so hot
And it hurts my head a lot.

I had a Slush Puppy and it was made out of ice
I decided it was time to see the mice
After that
My tummy became fat!

So that's all
I've got to go to the mall.

Eva Mannan (9)
Highlands Primary School

Fireworks

Fireworks, fireworks are colourful
They look as if they were there.
Fireworks, fireworks are very bright
They give out a lot of light.

Fireworks, fireworks everywhere
People cheering here and there.
Fireworks, fireworks sparkle in the sky
Fireworks, fireworks twinkle up high.

Fireworks, fireworks come down here
Fireworks, fireworks don't go up there.
Fireworks, fireworks are very hot
Fireworks, fireworks help us a lot.

Heena Bashir (10)
Highlands Primary School

The Sun

The sun is there,
The sun is bright,
The sun is the happiest, it gives us light.

The sun is bright,
The sun is there, it brings us sunshine,
It shines so clear.

The sun is bright, it brings us light,
It gives us a positive thought,
It is really bright.

Faraz Bashir (9)
Highlands Primary School

The Lovely Beach

I went to the beach one hot summer's day
And built a castle in the sand.
The waves then began to sway,
In the sea I lost my band.
The waves were rough
And the tides were tough.
The wind was blowing,
The clouds were showing.
Oh, we had to go home!
But I had a lovely beach day
And I say it was a beautiful sight,
As we went home
In the ever-fading light.

Seshani Sritharan (9)
Oaklands School

The Crazy Zoo

What a crazy zoo!
The tiger brought a cup of tea
For the man in the cage.
The spider served cakes
For you and me.
The elephant got his wage.
The snakes cleared the bugs off the floor.
The lions then prepared the meal.
The monkey said to give the humans more.
The seals made all the deals.
What a crazy zoo!

Victoria Armitage (9)
Oaklands School

The Lazy Lion

He yawned and showed his big, white teeth
And then went back to sleep again.
How could this lion be so tired?
The king of the jungle, so boring?

He yawned and opened his big, yellow eyes
And stretched his body out so wide.
What would his appetite be today?
What would be his favourite prey?

He yawned and lay on his back
And dreamt of a zebra leg.
Would he show his fierce roar?
Would he show his great speed?

The answer was yes
The king of the beasts was about to rise.

Matilda Brookes (9)
Oaklands School

Me And Maya At The Seaside

Me and my sister, Maya, went down the steps
And at the seaside we were digging.
We went in the water, cold and clear
And caught some crabs under the pier.
We heard the waves crashing and screeching
With the children playing like mad.
We ate our lunch until we were full.
I had a hunch we'd catch some fish
And serve it to Mummy on a silver dish.
Maybe Mummy will think it's delicious,
The best she will ever see,
The reason why? Simple!
It was caught by Maya and me!

Jasmine Osmani (9)
Oaklands School

The Seaside

The waves were swaying softly on the beach
Then I heard a great big screech
A dad was teaching his son to sail
A dog jumped up wagging his tail.

The sea was rough and crashing on the rocks
A sweet little girl with golden locks
Was playing in the sand for the rest of the day
Until she joined her friends and went away.

Georgia Lester (9)
Oaklands School

The Peckish Penguin

Penny is a peckish penguin
She likes to eat and munch the fish
She'll even eat your peanut butter sandwiches.
Penny is a peckish penguin
She likes to swim and jump about
But best of all
She likes to eat your peanut butter sandwiches.

Isabella Sawtell (9)
Oaklands School

Terrible Tigers

Tigers are playing, having fun,
Jumping and prancing in the sun.
Keeper bringing lots of meat,
What's in store? What's their treat?
Then the tigers start to bite,
Really, what a terrifying sight!

Tigers are playing, having fun,
Jumping and prancing in the sun.

Tabitha Aiken (8)
Oaklands School

Seaside

Sailing by the seaside shore
What fun it is sitting on a sandy floor
Sailing by the seaside shore
Eating cakes, wanting more.

Running by the seaside shore
Feeling the sand between my toes
Running by the seaside shore
Watching the gulls sitting in rows.

Splashing in the seaside waves
I look at my mum and give her a wave
She calls, 'Shall we go for a swim?'
We run and jump right in.

Swimming in the seaside waves
Mum and I are having fun
We run out and lie in the sun
Soon the day will be done.

Tia Lineker (8)
Oaklands School

My Magical Day

I went into the woods one night
And something gave me a fright.
There it was, a little elf,
'Would you like some tea?' said he.

I went through the trees
And saw magical bees.
Then there we were,
We had reached his world.

There were fountains and ponds
And silvery swans,
Fishes flipping in the sea
And unicorns with glowing horns.

Roberta Kent (8)
Oaklands School

Seaside

Running on the hot, sandy dunes
Racing down a huge, burning hill
Snorkelling underwater looking at the fish
Suddenly a stingray fish in sight
I swim before I get a bite.

Running through the cold, wet waves
Suddenly I see a cave
I run to discover its secrets
Captured by pirates, I feel very brave
One pirate says, 'You're our slave.'

Running back out in the sun
Running fast to find my mum
There she is sitting on the sand
She holds out her arms, I grab her hand.

Grace Cambridge (8)
Oaklands School

A Snowy Night

I went to the woods one snowy night,
And something scary gave me a fright.

I ran back home and went to my bed,
I said to myself, *where is my ted?*

Then I found my ted and rested my eyes
For thirty seconds, then I opened my eyes.

I dressed up warm and I went to the park,
I saw something spooky, but it was dark.

I glared at it, trying to think, what is that?
But behind the tree I found a little cat.

I said hello
And the cat said nothing, not even hello.

Benita Kaur Bahra (7)
Oaklands School

Magical Poetry

I went into the wood one windy night
And something gave me a fright.

There I was, I lost my way
And squirrels squeaked along the path.

Then I saw a fountain, so sparkly and dark,
Fairies came and sang a song
And then they came along.

Katie Andrews (7)
Oaklands School

The Terrific Tiger

Roaming through the jungle is the terrific tiger,
Stripes bulging black and orange, so bright.
Creeping through the trees, looking for the prey to kill.
There is a little deer,
Terrific tiger pounces perfectly,
He has found his dinner today.

Megan Huggins (8)
Oaklands School

Spooky Poetry

I went into the wood one day,
Then I saw the trees sway.

I lost my shoe on the way,
Then I saw shiny fountains sparkling away.

Then I saw lots of trees and so many leaves,
Then I saw colourful glitter coming down the trees.

But I don't know if I saw toadstools or mushrooms,
But now I want to see magical fairies and unicorns.

Sonia Bhangal (8)
Oaklands School

The Magical Wood

I went to the wood one stormy night,
I saw witches and their cats fall with fright.

Then I heard something whimpering, it made me jump,
I walked over and sat on a lump.

I saw sly foxes staring at the ground,
All of a sudden they started to pound.

I couldn't feel the lovely breeze,
Then I started to freeze.

I fell into the sparkling stream,
With fairies all around me.

They sang to me, I fell asleep,
Up the stairs the witches creep.

Was it a dream?
I think it was.

Harriet Davies (7)
Oaklands School

The Seaside

Dogs are barking up and down
Seagulls screech on the windy beach
Ice cream dripping down my face
I get up quick and join a race.

Dogs are barking up and down
Children playing together
Sandcastles here and there
Bouncy balls in the air.

Amber Preston (8)
Oaklands School

My Magical Poem

I went into the wood one day,
There the trees were in my way.

Then a little creature came up to me,
'Come and have some tea,' said he.

I went through some trees
And saw magical bees.

I sang a song,
The time wasn't so long.

There was a blossom tree
That made me smile with glee.

There I was woken up from my dream,
I struggled back down, wanting to dream in a stream.

There I was at home,
With my dog eating his bone.

Abbie Hembury (7)
Oaklands School

Magical Poetry

I went into the woods one sunny day
And there I was, I lost my way.

I saw a rabbit all fluffy and white
And her teeth were really bright.

I saw a bird singing a song
And the song was very long.

I saw kittens playing
And I said, 'I'm staying!'

Zara Rashid (7)
Oaklands School

Fairy Tale

I went into the wood one night
And gosh, I had an awful fright.

There were bats, witches and fairies
Wearing odd hats.

Then I stopped what I was doing,
To listen to the fairies singing.

Also I could hear the trees,
Blowing in the nice soft breeze.

Then the fairies started singing louder
And I fell asleep.

Was it a dream?
I think so.

Olivia Singer (8)
Oaklands School

The Weird Woods

I went into the woods one day
And I saw a fish jumping away.

I looked at the light
And it gave me a fright.

I saw a tree, it was talking
And it frightened me when it started walking.

I saw a rabbit hop from a fox,
I might have been walking into a magical box.

Alexandra Williams (7)
Oaklands School

Talking Animals

I went into the wood one windy night
And something lurking gave me a fright.

I saw an old man who gave me a glare
And said, 'You don't want to go over there, there's a lair.'

I turned around and saw a fish,
He said, 'Come over here, there's lots of talking things.'

I saw loads of ponds and silvery swans
And overhead, fairies with wands.

There were friendly foxes, friendly things,
Friendly bears, friendly hares.

I walked on by and saw a cat and dog playing
And I said, 'I'm staying!'

Alexis Shore (8)
Oaklands School

The View Of The Zoo

I went to the zoo with my mum and dad
I looked at the gorilla, what a big lad!
He had a big, hairy coat which was thick
And played quietly with a nearby stick.
Then he looked at me with a menacing glare
All I could do was sit there and stare.
Then he stared back with his tiny little eyes
And then I knew this animal was wise.

Phoebe Gibbons (8)
Oaklands School

The Magic Wood

I went into the wood one day
And there I was and lost my way.

Then I saw an old lady, black and white
And she gave me a big fright.

Then I saw a unicorn,
With a multicoloured horn.

I saw a tree with a nose, mouth and eyes
And it always tells lies.

What about the weird creatures in the sky?
They may be mean, bye-bye.

Emily Galman (7)
Oaklands School

Paw Prince

Coming out of nowhere,
Her fur blows in the winds,
Crystal clear snow,
Cold as ice,
As far as the eye can see.
She turns her head
And looks around,
Her white fur touches the snow,
As she cautiously steps forward,
Her call echoes in the cold night air
As it weaves itself through the mountains.
Thousands of scents, each one different,
Blowing through the cold, icy air,
She turns around,
Disappearing once more.

Abbi Wren (11)
Roydon Primary School

Magical Creatures

I used to believe there was another land
For different creatures
Other than man.
Ghosts and goblins,
Witches too,
Werewolves that howl
On the night of full moon.
Pixies, fairies, elves and gnomes
Pumpkins lit outside of homes.
Spells, chants, potions and all
Covens and a crystal ball.
Leprechauns, ogres, giants and more
Vanquished demons that die with a roar.
Another place, full of magic
But if it gets to your head
Then it could be tragic!
So is this a myth
Or is it really true?
I guess no one knows
Or maybe you do!

Ellie Woodriffe (10)
Roydon Primary School

Ill With A Cough

I've got a cough and cold
And I have lost my appetite,
But I've been told and told,
That I must take a bite.
Now finally I recover,
But will I ever discover,
That illness is not good
And eat vegetables, I should!

Theresa Dunthorne (8)
Roydon Primary School

The Scary Dragon

The dragon lurks in his cave all year
Only to come out if an intruder might appear.

The farmers, a warning never to mock
The dragon if you want to keep your crop.

If the dragon catches you, you can't outrun his speed
You'll just have to become his next nutritious feed.

Never mess with the dragon's fire
You'll soon learn it's hotter than lava!

The dragon's claws are as sharp as a knife
It very soon could take your life.

This warning goes out throughout the world
To put away your diamonds and pearls.

Antony Wren (9)
Roydon Primary School

My Best Friend

My best friend is covered in fur,
She woofs but doesn't purr.
She licks my ear,
As I love dear.
We talk and while we're on a walk,
My secrets she will never tell.
And she and I know each other so very well.
Our favourite game is fetch the ball,
She races to me when I call.
I wouldn't be without my friend,
We'll be together till the end.
With these clues I'm sure you've guessed,
That my best friend is my dog, Bess.

Rebecca Talbot (10)
Roydon Primary School

Cuddles And Me

Running in a cage,
Happy as can be,
Slurping really loud,
Cuddles and me.

Wheel spinning fast,
Climbs up bars,
Licking himself,
Cuddles and me.

Big, fat cheeks, storing food for later,
Only seen at night,
My long-haired hamster,
Cuddles and me!

Lucy Hancock (10)
Roydon Primary School

Sunsets

A yellow blaze,
From the sky above,
With fuchsia specks,
The colour of love.
And purple streaks,
In the colourful sky,
Golden spots like the moon,
As the sun bids me goodbye.
The moon shimmers palely,
The moon I've just met,
And the sky starts to darken,
As I watch the sunset.

Dana Moss (10)
Roydon Primary School

Why So Shy?

Sitting in the corner, nervous, anxious
Too scared and too shy to join in
Time passes by, lessons will fly.
They fly, fly away, but I'm still unable to say . . .
Anything.
Picking up my courage in a black leather suitcase,
Raising my hand to the sky,
The question is asked
But time flashes past. I didn't have the chance to speak.

A sigh of disappointment fills the room as I lower my hand,
Shy and scared again . . .

Katie Bees (10)
Roydon Primary School

Barking In Space

Pluto, always running round me
An icy-blue coat has
My little pal.
Smaller than all the others,
He circles me.
Moving far away but always coming back.
He is a mystery to all who gaze at him.
Night is his favourite time to play,
But should you blink or look away,
Too late, he's gone!
My pal, Pluto - the planet in the sky.

Connie Maunder (11)
Roydon Primary School

Opposites

I'm meant to be a devil
But I'm too good to be true,
I'm funny, angelic and kind,
But only kind for you.

I'm meant to be an angel,
But I'm too bad to be true,
I'm naughty, mischievous and fun,
But way too cool for you.

Hey, why don't we swap places?
Nobody will ever know.
Yah, good idea,
Let's get on with the show!

Dana McLean & Amy Hagues (10)
Roydon Primary School

Autumn Leaves

The ancient oak stands
Where many secrets lie,
Never to be found.
The crisp leaves sway gently in the wind,
Not knowing their fate,
That cruelly awaits them.
The oak watches the leaves,
As they twist and turn
And mutters, 'What's the world coming to?'
As the leaves bravely fall to their death.

Daniel Coss (11)
Roydon Primary School

Eragon

Eragon is the name courage
As swift as a sword
As wise as an owl
As kind as kind could be
But young like me
Living on the road

He rides a dragon
Named after her eyes
Sapphire, crystal-blue
For her scales gleam in the sunlight
Weapons thrice. She is.

Tail like a mace, deadly and sharp
Teeth as lethal as any sword
Talons as sharp as a knife
But gentle as a lamb
Talks through thoughts. To Eragon.

Brom is old and alone
His dragon gone. Slain by Morzon
Losing his powers. Age advances.
Eragon respects.
He grows and absorbs
Swordsmanship magic powers.

Brom leaves as Ra'zac's the monster Durza,
A shade of evil power. Into his body a
Dagger plunges.

Eragon our saviour, is alone.
Carries the fight in Alagaesia
In language old, pronouncing words
To help him overcome.

Thomas Behr (10)
Roydon Primary School

My Special Friend

My special friend is good to me
She's great, don't you see?
I look out for her.
She's kind it might occur,
We play together every day,
Her birthday's in the middle of May.
Every time I'm upset,
She'll give me a hug, I bet.
You see everyone needs a special friend,
To talk about each other's trends.

Mia Edgeworth (9)
Roydon Primary School

Crazy Maizy

Never naughty, never bad
Crazy Maizy is so mad.
Niggly and giggly and crazy is she
That's why we call her Crazy Maizy.
It's funny you see, she doesn't like daisies
She has a best friend, he's called Lee
But Crazy Maizy is too funny for me.

Olivia Harding (8)
Roydon Primary School

Daisy

Daisy is never sad, never mad, never bad.
She sits on a chair, sits on a table,
She never lets go of her teddy's label.
When she goes to school, she's never a fool.
She always looks after her little sister who is very tall.
Daisy likes to play with a ball.
Now it is time to go, bye-bye.

Katie Obeney (7)
Roydon Primary School

Mum's Poetry And About Her

It started just like this
Just a bit of fun
We thought it was funny
But we hardly knew what had just begun . . .

Then she started doing more
And went a bit crazy
We didn't help her
So we're a bit lazy

Then she couldn't stop
Something inside was lookin' for somethin' to do
The thing inside her she couldn't beat
So it must be something like kung fu

Now let me tell you
Poetry is a thing my mum loves
Let me tell you
Poetry is like two white doves

Let me tell you
My mum is cool
I've always loved her
And she absolutely rules

Let me tell you about my mum
She is sweet
She is kind and helpful
And she's got smelly feet

Also my mum
Likes to greet
Have sweets
And eat meat

My mum helps me out
We both like sheep which have fur
They're all fluffy
And are sweet just like her.

Niamh Carroll (8)
St Bedes RC Primary School, Chadwell Heath

The Cherry Blossom Village

Along around the world-o
Where most church bells go *ting!*
Is the Cherry Blossom Village
Deep inside Beijing.

Outside this lovely city
People have no clue
That the Cherry Blossom Village
Is what is underneath your shoe.

Who lives inside this paradise?
You ask. Well, let me see
Elves, pixies and fairy folk
I'm certain, not *maybe*.

So now you know along the world-o
Where rock and pop stars sing
Is the Cherry Blossom Village
Deep inside Beijing.

Shona Galt (7)
St Bedes RC Primary School, Chadwell Heath

Fairies, Magical Fairies

Fairies fly high in the sky
They come in the middle of the night
What a wonderful sight if you saw one tonight
You will be amazed at the colourful sight
Their wands twinkle ever so bright
Their wings help them fly all through the night
Oh, what a wonderful sight if I saw one tonight.

Mia Grant (7)
St Bedes RC Primary School, Chadwell Heath

My Hamster

I love my little hamster,
He's soft, cuddly and beige,
I gave him the name of 'Digger',
And he lives in his cage.

I love my little hamster,
With his twitchy, small, pink nose,
He wakes up at night,
But daytime he likes to doze.

Emma Tracy (7)
St Bedes RC Primary School, Chadwell Heath

Spiders

Spiders, spiders one by one
Spiders, spiders having loads of fun
Spiders, spiders come over here
I want to whisper something in your ear
Spiders, spiders look at your legs
They are bigger than pegs
Spiders, spiders very tall
But they can't even climb over the wall!

Beatrice Stanesby (10)
St James CE School, Harlow

Love

Love is like a princess singing in the rainbows
On a lovely day,
Looking through the windows,
How good it is to see your prince
Standing down below
Holding a bunch of flowers that smell so nice
With chocolates in his hand,
Cherry chocolates, oh how nice.
I know he must be the one,
As I see his lovely eyes.
I go downstairs to see him there,
He holds out a diamond ring
And asks me something . . .

Ellie Evans (8)
St James CE School, Harlow

Jewellery

Earrings, necklaces, bracelets too
Beads and bangles
Of green and blue.

Sparkling in my jewellery box
I hide it well
And it's away locked.

It is special to me and means so much
My little sister
Can never touch.

I love it so much and it's precious to me
It's my personal belongings
For no one to see.

Holly Angel (9)
St Katherine's CE Primary School, Canvey Island

Best Friends

Whenever I'm in a dilemma
I have always got my best friend, Emma
She is so kind and really great
She is definitely a girl's number one mate

We share our worries
And our fears
Our shoulders are always there
When one of us is in tears

She is such a laugh
To play out with
She is so much fun
She is my best friend
My number one!

Jessica Lee (11)
St Katherine's CE Primary School, Canvey Island

Love

What is it like, to be in love?
All those wonderful feelings
It's just a dream come true
The whole world's frozen, nothing matters anymore
It's like floating on a cloud, in your own world
Devotion, passion, lust is love
Like Cupid has just shot one of his golden arrows
Through my heart
Love is a secret, locked in a box
The key never to be found . . .

Rhiannan Crace (10)
St Katherine's CE Primary School, Canvey Island

Mystery Creature

I am like a graceful swan
That swiftly moves upon the lake
As proud as a king, as free as a dove
A precious creature that is in love
I look from place to place looking for care
But all I find is people acting not fair
No one knows who I am
I am the only one of my kind.

Reyad Nsimbi (11)
St Katherine's CE Primary School, Canvey Island

Heartbroken

Alone and miserable in the darkness you weep.
In bed you are comfortless, wishing to sleep.
Desolate and forlorn and wretched and cold,
An arrow pierced through your heart, the years getting old.
Helpless and cheerless and worried and sad,
Feeling like you're in a room that is driving you mad!

Jessica Gale (10)
St Katherine's CE Primary School, Canvey Island

Petrified

I froze
Not knowing what to do.
The wind howled through the doorways
Then I heard it . . . *wwooooo*
My skin was as cold as a stone,
My blood stopped running,
I was paralysed, fossilised.
My heart tried to leap out,
Then I heard footsteps . . .

Daniel Tudor (11)
St Katherine's CE Primary School, Canvey Island

Welly Boots

I love the wild, wet, windy days
Of rain and slushy sleet
For it's then I fetch my Wellingtons
I mean my rubber jellibongs, oh dear
I mean my webbingtons
And pull them on my feet

My sister, Jenna, hates rainy days
The cold makes her cry
But I've got my wellinbots
Oh dear, I mean my wellingots
To keep me warm and dry

But isn't it a nuisance
Isn't it a shame?
That though I love you
Wellibongs
I just can't say your name!

Georgia Plumb (9)
St Katherine's CE Primary School, Canvey Island

Winter

In winter stands a lonely tree,
Leaves dropping to the ground.
The wind whirls around me,
Whistling to the sky.
Snow crunches under my boots' footprints.
Everywhere snowflakes, white,
Wash the rooftops.
Birds have vanished one by one,
Flying away to find the sun.

Mollie Buckle (10)
St Katherine's CE Primary School, Canvey Island

Monday's Child Is Red And Spotty

Monday's child is red and spotty,
Tuesday's child won't use the potty.
Wednesday's child won't go to bed,
Thursday's child won't be fed.
Friday's child breaks all his toys,
Saturday's child makes an awful noise.
And the child that's born on the seventh day,
Is a pain in the neck like the rest, *OK?*

Erin Newman (7)
St Katherine's CE Primary School, Canvey Island

Calm

I'm as free as a bird,
As swift as it flies,
I'm as relaxed as a holiday
And I'm holding my head high.
I have nothing worrying me today,
While I'm out in the sun dreaming while I lay.
But now I'm as hungry as a tramp
And I'm getting hot in front of this lamp.
I am really hungry, I do not lie,
So I will now go and eat a cream pie.

Connor Plumb (11)
St Katherine's CE Primary School, Canvey Island

Shame

S econd day since it happened
H im not me
A disgrace for my family
M e in boiling hot water
E mbarrassed and expelled.

Jack Saunders (10)
St Katherine's CE Primary School, Canvey Island

Anger

Anger is like a volcano erupting all over a land
A river outraged on a country, drowning it into the depths
Like boiling hot water burning as hot as it will burn
Like a raging monster destroying its cage into a million pieces
Like a bomb exploding then a blood boil bursting
A big sting and then it is calm
And silent
And you are normal again.

Alex Bowhay (11)
St Katherine's CE Primary School, Canvey Island

Laughter

There was a boy with tears on his face
Because he was laughing with all of his mates

But over the road were some people giggling
And there was a girl who couldn't help dribbling

Then it was time to go back to school
With all of his mates thinking they're cool

The boy started to get a little left out
He looked like a doughnut for then and for now.

Curtis Cramp (11)
St Katherine's CE Primary School, Canvey Island

Anger

Anger is like a volcano, bitterness
Mad feelings, raging seas
And madness like a tiger roaring in your head
Like a thunderstorm with lightning
As hot as fire and the Earth's core.

Connor Garrett (10)
St Katherine's CE Primary School, Canvey Island

Heartbroken

I heard the news and suddenly felt a strong wind of hatred
A bullet flew straight through my heart
I didn't know if it was true so I just waited and waited
Then I heard footsteps,
I felt like a snail crushed on the side of the road
I was miserable, cheerless, lonely
I wanted to run into a dark room and slam the door shut.
Then the door opened . . .
I was heartbroken.

Abbie Toogood (10)
St Katherine's CE Primary School, Canvey Island

At The Stables

Hear the stable teachers calling different instructions to the riders.
Hear the clattering of hooves going batter-boom, batter-boom,
Like a sudden clap of thunder.
Hear the whinnying of horses in their stables.

Feel the soft, smooth, silky coat of the horses' and ponies' backs
As you stroke them.
Feel the different textures of the dandy brush, the metal comb
And the hoof pick.

Smell the sweet, sharp hay.
Smell the slow burning manure.
Smell the blended aromas of different horses and ponies.
Smell the feed from the cold metal feed room.

See four to eight horses and ponies in the arena.
See the stable instructors dotted around the stable yards.
See the horses and ponies hang their heads over the stable doors.
See the cars coming through the big, black, metal gates,
Bringing riders for their lessons . . .
At the stables.

Caitlin Smith (8)
St Thomas of Canterbury RC Primary School, Grays

Football

F ootwork is a big problem for me
O h no, my foot's stuck in the mud
O h no! the ball's gone over the wall
T oo many want to play
B oys shouting at me
A way players very rough
L oud cries when we score a goal
L ots of girls screaming at the goalie

I n the mud, worms have got earmuffs on
S ome guy's dancing about trying to get people's attention

F ull of nose bleeds and cuts
U nderground moles bounce about
N ow I think it's no fun at all!

Erin Rydings (10)
St Thomas of Canterbury RC Primary School, Grays

Happy Day

The sun is out,
The skies are blue,
I sat and wondered,
What to do.

My friend came round,
And asked to play,
And so I had,
A happy day!

Daisy Manning (9)
St Thomas of Canterbury RC Primary School, Grays

I Wake Today

I wake today
Get out of my bed,
Then stretch and yawn
And scratch my head.

I get my clothes
I put them on,
Whilst stifling another yawn.

I grab my breakfast
Bar of fuel,
Take my bag
And head to school.

When I arrive
I'm alarmed,
The lights are off
The doors are locked.

I check my phone
It's me, not them,
I woke too soon
It's 2am!

Darlletta Oduntan (10)
St Thomas of Canterbury RC Primary School, Grays

Fifth Of November

Remember, remember, the fifth of November
When fireworks go off and your clothes are all soft.
All the coloured fire sets our hearts' desire.
Remember, remember, the fifth of November.

Louisa Johnson (9)
St Thomas of Canterbury RC Primary School, Grays

My Best Friends

One is Kathleen,
She is really clean,
She is our mum at school,
Although she is really cool.

She is still my best friend!

Another is Daisy,
She is never lazy,
But sometimes she can be crazy,
Her nickname is Maisy.

She is still my best friend!

Then there's George,
We call him Porge,
He is very sporty,
But also naughty.

He is still my best friend!

You can't forget Mary,
She can be very dary,
She is a bit scary,
She looks like Halle Berry.

She is still my best friend!

Also Hannah,
She is forever eating a banana,
She can be very cheeky,
But she is very pretty.

She is still my best friend!

Then there is Elsie,
She looks a bit elfy,
She is really arty
And she can party.

She is still my best friend.

I have many other friends,
But it all depends,
If they are truly
My best friends!

Georgia Akhigbe (10)
St Thomas of Canterbury RC Primary School, Grays

All About Me

When I was in my mother's womb
She didn't stand a chance
She thought I was a boy
And nearly called me Lance

When I was in preschool
It was the best
I made one friend
Instead of the rest

When I was in reception
My friendship was gone
Not only I had no friends
It went down to none

Now let's go through the years
One, two, three, four, five and six
It is so cool
I don't play with sticks

Now I am in Year 6
I have loads of friends
By the time I am done
It won't be the end.

Catherine Abbott (10)
St Thomas of Canterbury RC Primary School, Grays

Monkey Business

Watch them swing,
Hear them shout,
You're sure to know
Who's about!

Swinging through the trees,
Dancing in the leaves,
Jumping up and down,
Monkeying around.

Bananas everywhere,
They never want to share,
But I do really care
About their welfare.

Eleanor Baker (7)
St Thomas of Canterbury RC Primary School, Grays

My Cat

I've got a cat called Spice
He makes me very happy
My mum likes him catching mice
I've had him since he was a baby
But he never wore a nappy!

I make him purr when I stroke his fur
He cries with delight when I feed him meat
He miaows and jumps on the computer seat
He licks his paws, then his feet.

At night he curls up on my pillow
Right next to my head
I adore my cat
My heart beats with joy
When I see him waiting on the mat.

Nicole Young (9)
St Thomas of Canterbury RC Primary School, Grays

The Big Fun Run

Today is the day to have some fun
So let's all go on the fun run
We raise money for the poor
We need to raise more and more
We were about to start the run
But the man did not have his gun
'I am so sorry for all this trouble,' he said
'I think I left it by my bed
I will just pop back and get it if you don't mind
Or we can go to the shops and see what we can find'

I found it he said in his head
He was right, it was right by his bed
All the runners felt very sad
One of them said, 'You are really bad.'
'I am sorry, I will make it up to you
How about tomorrow we go to the zoo?
I will pay, don't you worry
Then after we can have a curry.'
'Oh, thank you,' said the leader
'I bet you are a very good feeder.'

In the end they went to the zoo
They saw an elephant and a monkey too
'Thank you,' said the leader, 'I will pay
Maybe I will see you another day.'
'Of course you will,' the old man said
'Oh well, I'd better be off, I am off to bed.'
So remember when you do a fun run
That it is always the best way to have some fun.

Rebecca Mills (10)
St Thomas of Canterbury RC Primary School, Grays

The Dragon

Burning *t*rees with his fiery nostrils
He has powerful *h*ind legs to help him take off
Watch out everyone, here he comes

Doing a strange *d*ance in the night
Huge, *r*ound eyes
A long tail streaming behind him
Great wings of red and gold
Look at his shiny *c*oat of scales
But everyone hates him, *n*obody likes him.

Miriam Woodburn (9)
St Thomas of Canterbury RC Primary School, Grays

Winter Poem

F rosty flying reindeer fly on Christmas Eve
R eindeer love flying with Santa on Christmas Eve
E skimos go fishing on Christmas Eve
E lephants stay at home on Christmas Eve
Z ebras zoom home after shopping
I   cicles form on rooftop gutters
N oses are red and nights are longer
G ardens get full of snow in winter.

Marcus Cordery (7)
St Thomas of Canterbury RC Primary School, Grays

Christmas Fun

Christmas, Christmas is full of fun,
Presents and laughter all day long.
Santa is happy to see all the children
Sleeping soundly in their beds at night.

Boxing Day is still full of fun,
Children are sad because Christmas is over.
But new toys to play with and leftover turkey!

Charley Baker (7)
St Thomas of Canterbury RC Primary School, Grays

Seasons' Meanings

The winter's wind blows so hard,
The spring's growth warms your heart,
The autumn taunts,
The summer's warmth,
Some say they are the seasons' feelings
I say they are the seasons' meanings.

Josef Oliver (10)
St Thomas of Canterbury RC Primary School, Grays

Poems

Poems are great and fun to write
I love reading them, especially at night
When I'm finished I close my eyes tight
And don't wake up till it is light
I brush my teeth until they are white
And think what poem I will read tonight.

Ellie Beard (8)
St Thomas of Canterbury RC Primary School, Grays

Dolphins

Dolphins, dolphins, jumping in the air,
One called Jake, one called Amy
And one called Claire.
Fat, big, small, thin and long,
Four of them are singing a song.

One day dolphins I saw,
I gave them food, some wanted more.
Even some came up to the shore.
These lovely creatures from the blue
Were they the best things from the sea?
Who knew?

Sophie Kanikuru (8)
St Thomas of Canterbury RC Primary School, Grays

A Special Brother

My brother is a dream,
But we are never a team.
He kicks me in the morning,
So I give him a warning.
He never cooks me food,
I think he's very rude.
He never gives me a kiss,
So I will give him this . . .

Laura Grace (10)
St Thomas of Canterbury RC Primary School, Grays

In My Dream

In my dream I saw
The stunning Labrador's coat,
Gleaming in the golden sun
Of August's summer breeze.

In my dream I heard
The extreme sound of tornadoes wailing,
In the height of the hurricane,
Moving steadily along tornado valley.

In my dream I could taste
The wonders of a thin, crispy Margherita pizza,
Served with hot, soft garlic bread.

In my dream I could touch
A robin resting gently on my finger,
It was so relaxed and not frightened.

In my dream I could smell
The salty chips and burger,
As my teeth enjoyed the taste of McDonald's.

In my dream I saw
The Arsenal play sensationally well,
Winning against champs Chelsea 4-3.

Matthew Payne (11)
Scotts Primary School

In My Dream

In my dream I saw
Fields of icing flowers,
Trees full of money and red and pink candy canes,
The sun - a bright yellow gobstopper in the sky.

In my dream I smelt
The sugary sky,
Sherbet lemon,
And melted, milky chocolate
As it rained down in the distance.

In my dream I heard
The twittering song of a chocolate bird,
The croaking of a slimy, sherbet frog,
The ear-piercing screams of the happy gingerbread children
Collecting pink, blue, green, red, yellow, purple and orange
Gummy worms from the soil.

In my dream I saw
The candy canes jumping joyously off the trees,
The satisfactory lemonade lake shimmering in the sun,
The rock pools; lemonade trickling down to the lake,
Buzzing bees everywhere! A trail of sherbet behind them.

In my dream I saw
The fish swimming symmetrically like they're putting on a show
In the lemonade water,
The sherbet clouds through the blue sky.

In my dream I saw
Gingerbread houses so small and cute,
The trees shaking hands in the wind.

In my dream I saw
Horses running with horns on their foreheads,
Sparkling sherbet dust, magical and unique . . .

Jordan Howell (10)
Scotts Primary School

In My Dream

In my dream I saw
A blackbird soar above,
Sweeping high and sweeping low,
I suddenly started to float!

In my dream I smelt,
The yellow, shining sherbet sand,
I'm suddenly in a candy land!
Gingerbread as a house
And I quickly gobble a chocolate mouse!

In my dream I tasted,
The sweet lemonade in the water fountains
And the stripy candy canes,
Swinging on the chocolate bar swings,
Like the little toddlers in the park.

In my dream I saw
A blackbird soar above,
Oh no, not again, whatever will happen next?

I'm not in my dream anymore,
I'm back at home,
On my comfy bed,
Didn't I just have the best dream yet?

Esme Ware (11)
Scotts Primary School

In My Dream

In my dream I saw
A dull day - windy, rainy weather
Making gloomy faces go grey.

In my dream I heard
The pittering raindrops
Collide against the floor
Coming down harder
Through force.

In my dream I saw
Myself walk out the front door
Into chocolate rainfall.

In my dream I heard
Myself get sucked up
Into the high sky.

In my dream I saw
Myself appear in Candyland
With bright colours, everything edible
And little animals, trudging on sweet, sugared grass.

In my dream I heard
Myself get shaken by a terrifying earthquake
That was when I got awoken
By my alarm clock
Flashing and vibrating.

Megan Willis (10)
Scotts Primary School

In My Dream

In my dream I saw
A fearsome, fiery dragon
Swoop silently over the red volcano
Spitting burning bubbles
Casting bright lights over the clouds.

In my dream I heard
The crashing thunder
And the crunching lightning
Cursing the evil sunlight.

In my dream I saw
A sleek leopard
Throw its claws over the weary tree.

In my dream I heard
The pitter-patter of a spotted ladybird
Gathering tasty treats
For its young
Small as a raindrop.

In my dream I saw
A chocolate palace
Drizzled in creamy-white ice cream.

In my dream I heard
A werewolf howling
Like an ocean liner
Crying angry calls to the glowing moon.

In my dream I saw
A peaceful lake
Rippling at a touch
Creating a million homes
For birds for years to come.

Rosie Howard (10)
Scotts Primary School

In My Dream

In my dream I saw,
The moon shining like fire at a scorching temperature,
As it put the spotlight on me.

In my dream I gazed at,
The screeching members of the public with signs and messages,
As I walked to the end
Of a deep, dark, gloomy cliff.

In my dream I felt,
The winter wind on my back,
As I lifted my arms
Into the night sky.

In my dream I heard,
The boys cry in sadness
And the girls laugh in happiness.

In my dream I stopped and stared at
Computer generated people,
Walking through each other
With ease.

In my dream I felt,
A bony hand grasp
My back and push me,
Into mid-air.

In my dream I heard,
The wind turning stronger,
As I opened my eyes
Into a pit of despair.

In my dream I heard,
The sound of a snap,
As I fell into the unknown.

Jonathan Wake (11)
Scotts Primary School

In My Dream

In my dream I was on
A large, round, red roundabout
Spinning round and round like a hamster on his wheel.

In my dream I felt
My brown, wide eyes open,
The sound of the whistling wind,
Singing a lullaby.

In my dream I saw
The red ball of fire peeping through
The fluffy clouds, glazing secretly in the tall, green trees.

In my dream I heard
The pitter-patter of
The soft, sweet pear drops
Falling from the bright sky.

In my dream I reached for
The baby-pink, silky flower petal
As the pearl-white raindrops
Ran down the green stem.

In my dream I saw
The rainbow-coloured butterflies
Soaring around the starlight, golden sun.

Leona Holland (11)
Scotts Primary School

In My Dream

In my dream
I saw myself resting on a swing all alone
Gradually moving, staring at the gritty, grey gravel.

In my dream
I heard fluttering birds tweeting
And my swing screeching like a piece of white, dusty chalk
Writing on a blackboard.

In my dream
I could taste the warm toast being smothered
In raspberry jam.

In my dream
I could feel my brown, curly hair
Blowing against my back.

In my dream
I tiptoed away from this spooky something,
But what?

Jasmine Elliston (11)
Scotts Primary School

A Bright Night

One star passing by my house,
The others just twinkling.
This amazing show seemed so close,
It looked like the stars were able to dance and sing.
The stars went to sleep
As the daylight drew in.
The sun started to rise,
Another new day full of surprise.

Rosie Stowe (8)
Thorpedene Junior School

Christmas

C hildren opening their lovely presents
H olly on the door
R eindeer flying in the air
I cing on the Christmas cake
S now is falling down from the sky
T ree is full of decorations
M aking a snowman
A ngels flying in the sky
S nowman made of snow.

Carmen Ng (11)
Thorpedene Junior School

Got To Get To School!

School is waiting,
I can't be late,
Hurry, hurry,
It's half-past eight.
Out the door
And down the street,
Then quietly, quietly
Take your seat.

Kirsty Whitfield (10) & Paige Lewis (11)
Thorpedene Junior School

Netball

N ets up high
E veryone enjoys it
T eams are always equal
B alls always used
A ttack is working well
L istening to the rules
L et's play to the end of the day!

Hannah Vinten (9)
Thorpedene Junior School

Night Of The Pegasus

During the night
At a horse's home
My horse had a fright
Cos it was all on its own
When I looked in the stable
My horse was asleep
Shhh little pony
Do not peep

I looked at the stars
That were way far
Then I remembered
The Pegasus myth
I say it's true but others
'As if I believed in it!'

So I look up
And see a shooting star
Off to the telescope
Can't see, it's too far

From the stable
I escape
I look through the telescope
Is that a horse with a cape?

It's a Pegasus
I knew it was true
No one will believe me
So what will I do?

I won't tell them
But now morning has come
Last night was so much fun
I will tell my horse, he won't believe his eyes
But all I can say is
Last night was a surprise!

Paige Martin (10)
Thorpedene Junior School

In The Winter

In the winter
The fox stays in its den
In the winter
The cat sleeps in front of the fire
In the winter
The hedgehog hibernates
In the winter
I sleep in my bed
In the winter
It's cold
In the winter
The leaves come off the trees
That's what happens
In the winter.

Ella Osborne (8)
Thorpedene Junior School

My Cat Is A . . .

M ischief
Y awning

C ute
A ttached to me
T ickly

She is sensitive, silly, organised
And a very clawy, untidy, tiny, educated animal,
And a cuddly, nutty, detective,
Her ears are edged and she purrs.

Elisha Caddell (8)
Thorpedene Junior School

The Lonely, Dead Tree

I'm a lonely, dead tree
I'm as sad as can be

I play in a boat
Because I can't float

I've got an old trunk
And I smell like a skunk

I'm like a slimy slug
And I crawl like a bug

I've got two brollies
And I like to eat lollies

I've got a big nose
It's alright I suppose

I'm very wise and old
And my roots are full of mould

I'm a lonely, dead tree
I'm as sad as can be.

Rebecca Bailey (11)
Thorpedene Junior School

The Seasons

The spring is where the blossom starts,
Summer's getting closer.
It's autumn time at last,
Now winter's coming nearer.
The nights are getting longer,
Back to spring at last.

Zac Sussex (7)
Thorpedene Junior School

Snow Is Falling!

Snow is falling
What a delight!
It's snowing, it's snowing
We can go out and play.
It's snowing, it's snowing
Come out and say
'It's snowing, it's snowing
Hip hip hooray!'

Bethany Lewis (7)
Thorpedene Junior School

My Strange Brother

My brother is weird, my brother is strange
He really should be locked in a cage.
He howls in the middle of the night
He gives me the biggest fright.
My brother's nails are long and sharp
His yellow eyes sparkle madly in the dark.
My brother eats food for the dogs
He even eats hogs and frogs.
Now you know my brother is weird and strange
Do you think he should be locked in a cage?

Shannon Watson (11)
Thorpedene Junior School

Dolphins

Dolphins dive throughout the day
Make them swoop and swerve and play

See them dancing all around
See them prancing to the ground

Hear them clicking with their voices,
Love them all, they have no choices!

Olivia Marsh (8)
Thorpedene Junior School

Christmas

C hrist is born
H appy New Year's on its way
R eindeer pulling Santa's sleigh
I cicles hanging
S now is falling
T ree brightly decorated
M any presents being opened
A ngels are flying
S inging carol singers.

David Thomas (11)
Thorpedene Junior School

Puppies

Puppies are sweet
Puppies are cute
They can't wear dresses
Not even a suit
They can wear a coat
But not hat and scarf
They run in the mud
Then they need a bath!

Sarah Jayne Brewster (10)
Thorpedene Junior School

Swimming

S wimming is great, swimming is good.
W inning the swimming race
I 'm having fun
M y arms are aching
M y legs are tired
I want to give up
N o way am I going to stop
G o to swimming, it's brilliant!

Megan Smith (9)
Thorpedene Junior School

Rodger The Rabbit

Rodger the rabbit likes his habit,
He nibbles at carrots,
He hates parrots
And he lies in the straw
Eating more and more!
He has floppy ears,
I think he likes beers.
Rodger has a bushy tail
And he likes his nails.
Rodger the rabbit, he's my pet,
I think we need to take him to the vet!

Laura Joseph (8)
Thorpedene Junior School

My Brother, Logan

Logan is my brother,
Logan's so cute,
Sometimes he's cheeky,
Sometimes he's good.
He scratches our faces,
He's learning to stand without a hand,
I love my brother
And that's a fact.

Michaela Maya Benedetti (7)
Warley Primary School

Orange, Red And Yellow

Orange, red and yellow
Whatever can it be?
It's a candle showing me where to be.

Orange, red and yellow
Whatever can it be?
It's a candle burning brightly in the dark.

Orange, red and yellow
Whatever can it be?
A worn out candle dripping with wax as the hours go by.

Sophie Painter (8)
Warley Primary School

Recycle

There's pollution in the ocean,
Birds can't fly in the sky,
There's oil in the soil
And smoke on the oak.

Don't bin it,
They will just landfill it.
So recycle your paper and plants,
While you still have the chance.

Erin Thompson (8)
Warley Primary School

The Tiger

This poem's about me, I'm a mammal,
A tiger - that's my name,
Listen to what's been happening,
You'll hang your head in shame.

You're killing us - yes, humans!
More die every day,
We're badly endangered, you killers,
Do you want us to fade away?

Have you ever been caught in a skin-cutting snare
Or have you ever been shot?
You say it's not your fault for putting down traps,
But an accident it is not.

Three species are already extinct because of you,
For their fur that's orange and black,
Do you know how hurtful it feels,
To see it on a human's back?

We'll move on to something else now,
Something called our home,
You're cutting down our trees,
We now have less space to roam.

You've invaded our land,
New houses you've made,
There's no place to hide
And there's nowhere with shade.

There's no more deer,
There's nothing to eat,
If we don't die of hunger,
We'll die of the heat.

I don't want to be extinct,
But extinction's coming fast,
Our future is in your hands,
Don't let us be a thing of the past.

Emily Rush (10)
William Read Primary School

The Three Little Pigs Come To An End

There once lived three little pigs,
They lived with their mother who was fat and rather big.
The pigs drove her up the wall,
Surely she's had enough once and for all?

Then one day she said to them,
'It's time to leave your humble pig pen
And go out into the world on your own,
And please don't complain and start to moan!'

So they packed their bags without moaning or speaking
And opened the door with their water bottles hopelessly leaking.
They kissed and waved their mother goodbye,
Not knowing she had just made a blueberry pie!

They walked away not knowing the wolf was about,
The wolf eats pigs whole, including their tail and snout.
The pigs passed a shop with a sign saying, *'Do you pigs want to
learn how to fly?'*
Surely this distracted the pigs from the smell of home-made pie!

The pigs agreed to go in the shop,
In there they learned how to fly and they also bought themselves
a top!
They picked up their bags and started twirling their tails,
They flew through the air and over the gales!

But they did not know that the flight only lasted for five minutes!
The wolf knew this and waited for them silently in a pile of tins.
As the pigs were landing, they didn't know they were landing in
the wolf's tummy
And they went down his throat whole, as quiet as a bunny.

And that is the sad end to the three little pigs!

Rebecca Hayes (11)
William Read Primary School

What Am I?

I'm made of silk
But as white as milk
I can be any size
And catch flies

I'm out in the rain
And feel no pain
I glisten in the sun
But don't weigh a ton

I appear overnight
And give some people a fright
I can be brushed away in no time
And this is the end of my rhyme.

What am I?
A: a web.

James Smith (10)
William Read Primary School

Beware!

Beware of this bubbling potion,
You can't get it off with a lotion.
This potion is very mean,
Your neighbours won't be very keen.
It will make you very bad,
In the end you will turn quite mad.
So don't mess with me,
Otherwise a monster you will be!

Megan Blackwell (9)
William Read Primary School

Young Writers Information

We hope you have enjoyed reading this book - and that you will continue to enjoy it in the coming years.

If you like reading and writing poetry drop us a line, or give us a call, and we'll send you a free information pack.

Alternatively if you would like to order further copies of this book or any of our other titles, then please give us a call or log onto our website at
www.youngwriters.co.uk

Young Writers Information
Remus House
Coltsfoot Drive
Peterborough
PE2 9JX

(01733) 890066